An Introd

The Irish Civil War

An Introduction

to

The Irish Civil War

John O'Donovan

MERCIER PRESS

Dedication

To my parents

MERCIER PRESS

Cork

www.mercierpress.ie

© John O'Donovan, 2022

ISBN: 978-1-78117-806-5

978-1-78117-807-2 [Ebook]

Cover Design: Sarah O'Flaherty

A CIP record for this title is available from the British Library

Printed and bound in the EU.

CONTENTS

Acknowledgements: 7

Introduction   9

Phase 1

July – December 1922   31

Phase 2

December 1922 – May 1923   48

Controversy, Reprisal, and Execution

   During the Civil War   59

Biographies   87

Appendix   114

Bibliography   118

Index   120

Acknowledgements

Thanks to Gabriel Doherty for sowing the seed of this project. I acknowledge the assistance of Donal Ó Drisceoil, Mervyn O'Driscoll, and Andy Bielenberg in giving me space to think and write the bulk of this text before the 2020 lockdown. I must commend the sharp eye of Mary Feehan whose queries on my drafts have improved the text no end. Thanks to all my colleagues in UCC and friends for their support and encouragement of my research and writing. Lastly, I dedicate this book to my parents for supporting me for many years in my vocation!

Introduction

On 11 July 1921, a Truce came into effect, ending the fighting between the Irish Republican Army (IRA) and the British Army. Less than a year later, the IRA had split, and British guns and shells were being used to attack rebel positions at the Four Courts in Dublin. This marked the beginning of the Civil War, which lasted less than a year but whose effects are still being felt to the present day. How did the united nationalist front that held together during the War of Independence fall apart so quickly?

The Sinn Féin movement and the IRA that fought the War of Independence were not, as has been often suggested, a united and cohesive movement by the time of the Truce. IRA General Headquarters (GHQ) ordered every officer to remain on a war footing. It was known that tensions existed inside the IRA and between the IRA and the Republican government, theoretically in charge. Cathal Brugha, the Minister for Defence and Richard Mulcahy, the IRA chief-of-staff, were tasked with coordinating the overall strategies of the army.

In this they were, in theory, supported by Michael Collins, who as well as being Minister for Finance was also Director of Organisation and Intelligence at IRA GHQ. Collins' other role, however, was head of the Irish Republican Brotherhood (IRB) and thus of the Republic established by the IRB in 1867. In this role, he had the unswerving loyalty of IRB members in the government and the IRA.

Being the theoretical head of an alternative Republic, however, brought Collins into conflict with the leadership of the Republic declared at Easter 1916, especially the president of Dáil Éireann Éamon de Valera. While Collins professed loyalty to De Valera, it was a conditional loyalty. Although divisions went beyond personality clashes in the leadership of both Sinn Féin and the IRA, it was through the eyes of these personalities that the events after the War of Independence and before the Civil War came to be seen.

Further complicating the political picture was the position of the six of the nine Ulster counties which had been granted a parliament of their own under the Better Government of Ireland Act 1920. In the dying days of the War of Independence this parliament was opened by King George V in Belfast, and his appeal to 'all Irishmen to pause, to stretch out the hand of forebearance [sic] and conciliation' provided an opening for David Lloyd George, the British prime minister. Three days after the Truce came into effect, De Valera, along with Austin Stack, Arthur Griffith, Count George Plunkett, Robert Barton and Erskine Childers, met with Lloyd George at 10 Downing Street.

Lloyd George presented De Valera with a set of pro-posals for a peace settlement, which placed clear limits on any freedom sought by the Dáil president. The creation of the new northern Irish state took the 'Ulster Question' out of any potential settlement. Other obstacles presented included providing military and naval bases for British forces in the event of any resumption of a global war. Most disturbingly, for the more hard-line Republicans in the Dáil, was the proposal that any new Irish administration would have to swear an oath of allegiance to the British monarch.

De Valera rejected the proposals but agreed to keep dialogue with London open to avoid the prospect of a resumption of war. Having been re-elected president on 26 August 1921, he was authorised by his new cabinet to continue discussions. After tortuous negotiations by letter, a form of words was arrived at which would serve as a starting point for formal negotiations: 'how the association of Ireland with the community of nations known as the British empire may be best reconciled with Irish National Aspirations.'

Most people, inside and outside of the Dáil, assumed that De Valera would lead any negotiating team on behalf of the Irish Republic. This assumption, however, failed to consider his personal hesitations and his need to be seen to keep the voluble coalition that Sinn Féin had become together. The final delegation consisted of Griffith, Collins, Barton, Childers, George Gavan Duffy and Eamonn Duggan. Gavan Duffy and Childers had helped De Valera prepare a draft treaty, entitled 'Draft Treaty A', which embodied De Valera's ideas of 'external association' between the Irish Republic and the British empire. This was given to the delegates, or plenipotentiaries (a phrase that would cause controversy later), as the basis for opening the discussions with Lloyd George and his delegates.

Negotiations commenced at 10 Downing Street on 11 October 1921. Talks quickly boiled down to exchanges between Lloyd George and Winston Churchill (the Secretary for War) on one side, and Griffith and Collins on the other. Two issues were identified as the major obstacles: the precise constitutional status of a state governed from Dublin, and the future of the northern Irish state. In early November Lloyd George faced a domestic political crisis which led him to extract from Griffith personal assurances that the Irish delegates would accept an oath of allegiance to the crown and inclusion in the British empire. Any future government in Dublin would have to swear allegiance to the British Monarch as head of the 'community of nations known as the British Empire'. The exact wording was modified several times during the course of the talks, but the central fact remained: an Irish Republic was off the table.

That same crisis also gave the British prime minister an opportunity to pressure Griffith and Collins to accept a Boundary Commission which would define the boundary between Northern Ireland and the Dublin-governed state. This allowed Lloyd George to present to his Tory coalition partners a settlement of the issue of Northern Ireland, ensuring the coalition government of enough support in the House of Commons to continue in office.

Negotiations then moved to the subject of the precise constitutional status of any Dublin government. On 22

November, the Irish delegation drew up a memorandum in response to a draft treaty submitted by the British. The British treaty spoke of Dominion Status, the Irish memo argued for a form of External Association; each side rejected the proposals of the other. By this time, it was becoming clear to both Irish and British negotiators that Griffith was struggling to bring his colleagues with him.

Three days later Griffith and Collins attended a stormy meeting of the Dáil cabinet. Cathal Brugha clashed with both men over the reported progression of negotiations. The oath proposal was rejected, and Griffith undertook not to sign any document on behalf of the Irish people without prior consultation. While in Dublin, Collins also met with IRB colleagues to prepare for a resumption of war in case talks in London broke down.

Back in London Childers, Gavan Duffy and Barton began negotiations over a modified version of External Association. Collins' absence from these talks convinced Lloyd George to sit down with him on Monday 5 December. Both men covered a range of issues. Rumours by this stage were sweeping London and Dublin that the talks were on the point of failure.

Seizing this opportunity, Lloyd George theatrically threatened Griffith and Collins with immediate war unless the delegation agreed to treaty terms. Following several hours of discussion, the Irish delegation formally signed the 'Articles of Agreement for a Treaty between Great Britain and Ireland' in the early hours of Tuesday 6 December 1921.

The Irish delegates to the Treaty negotiations photographed at Hans Place London the morning after the signing of the Treaty, 7 December 1921 L-R Arthur Griffith, Ned Duggan, Erskine Childers, Michael Collins, George Gavan Duffy, Robert Barton and John Chartres.
(Illustrations from the Mercier Archive)

Immediate reaction to the signing of the 'Treaty', as it came to be popularly called, was one of relief and jubilation on both sides of the Irish Sea. Privately, however, the leaderships of Sinn Féin and the IRA were uneasy about the future unity of their movements based on the terms published in the press. A Dáil cabinet meeting was held upon the return of the delegation to Dublin on 7 December. There, more energy was spent debating and arguing how the Treaty was signed rather than discussing what was contained in it. De Valera, Brugha and Stack emerged as the three cabinet members most opposed to the Treaty for a variety of reasons. After rancour and personal insults had been traded, the vote was four to three in favour of accepting the Treaty although, as Stack pointed out, the delegates were under no obligation to support the Treaty, only to recommend it to Dáil Éireann.

Strong public debate on the Treaty had begun even before the Dáil met on 14 December 1921 and continued throughout the sittings in Dublin. The Roman Catholic hierarchy and, paradoxically, the IRB Supreme Council urged acceptance. De Valera argued publicly that its terms were 'in violent conflict with the wishes of the majority of this nation'. He was however careful to ask his supporters to refrain from violence: 'There is a definite constitutional way of resolving our political differences – let us not depart from it'. Tom Barry, the celebrated IRA commander in west Cork, wrote to the *Cork Examiner* contradicting a statement by Seán MacEoin that the Treaty 'gave him what he and his comrades had fought for.' Barry wrote:

> It is a misrepresentation of the ideal of every fighting man with whom I had been associated during hostilities. Not one man believed that the fight was being waged for other than the maintenance of the Irish Republic; not one of those (to my knowledge) who sacrificed their lives died for any other than the cause of the Irish Republic. (*Cork Examiner*, 21 Dec. 1921)

Shortly after eleven a.m. on 14 December Dáil Éireann's

debate on the Treaty commenced at rooms provided by University College Dublin at its premises on Earlsfort Terrace in Dublin. Eoin MacNeill occupied the speaker's chair: to his left sat De Valera, Brugha, Stack and their supporters; to his right sat Collins, Griffith and their supporters. Following opening public exchanges between Collins and De Valera (each man interrupted on several occasions) the opening days' debate was conducted in private. The chief question raised in the opening scenes was one repeated throughout: did the delegates in London exceed their brief in agreeing to the Treaty as presented before TDs?

Griffith and De Valera dominated the second public session, on 19 December. Griffith argued that the question before the Dáil was not a choice 'between an independent Republic and Dominion status. Rather it was between two forms of Association with the British Empire.' For his part, De Valera adapted Parnell's famous phrase uttered in 1885; pointing at Griffith, he declared: 'You are presuming to set bounds to the onward march of a nation.' The Treaty as presented, he concluded, 'does not do the fundamental thing. It does not bring us peace.' Austin Stack, following De Valera, was uncompromising: 'I stand for full independence, and nothing short of it.'

By 22 December, deputies had been speaking for and against the Treaty for eight days, and the stress and strain of such a physical investment was beginning to tell. Emotion was the hallmark of many of the speeches that day: speakers included Mary MacSwiney (sister of Terence),

Kathleen Clarke (widow of Tom) and Richard Mulcahy. MacSwiney asked if the TDs currently supporting the Treaty would have been elected the previous May if they had publicly supported then the terms they were supporting now. Clarke argued that the Treaty was 'a surrender of all our national ideals ... England's game of divide and conquer goes on.'

Dáil deputies returned from the Christmas recess on 3 January. Pro-Treaty TDs, buoyed by the public support expressed during the break, put forward an argument that the Treaty represented a stepping-stone to the desired Republic. Collins was central to this, arguing that the Treaty gave 'freedom ... not the ultimate freedom ... but the freedom to achieve it'.

This harked back to something he had written in the tumultuous early hours of 6 December 1921: 'what have I got for Ireland? Something she has longed for these past seven hundred years ... but will anybody be satisfied with it? Will anyone?' In a way, he was answering his own rhetorical question: people were supporting the efforts he and his colleagues had made, but not, to his mind, in enough quantities. While a desire for peace would probably see the Treaty passed by the Dáil (though the exact majority was uncertain), Collins was already looking forward to the battle for the hearts and minds of the Irish people.

Three more days of bitter debate followed, which showed that during its recess members of the Dáil had become more entrenched in their views. De Valera sought to play his trump card towards the end of the debate by

Éamon de Valera

Arthur Griffith

introducing his 'Document No. 2', the alternative to the Treaty which he had drafted, embodying and fleshing out his concept of External association with the empire. Because this concept would not meet with the approval of many TDs, De Valera withdrew the document from the debate. He then, on 6 January, offered his resignation as president of the Dáil. This tactic did not find favour with many on the pro-Treaty benches.

The following day the Dáil voted on the Treaty, after Griffith moved a motion calling for a vote. The result was sixty-four votes for, fifty-seven against. Whatever the motives of those who voted, and these have been the subject of some forensic scrutiny by contemporaries in their memoirs and later historians, the breach in the Sinn Féin movement was now clearly visible. Collins pleaded for unity, but the last word was left to his chief; De Valera rose to speak but had only uttered the phrase 'the world is looking on at us now …' before he was overcome and sank into his seat. One contemporary journalist wrote:

It was an awful moment. Women were weeping openly. Men were trying to restrain their tears. Some because of the approval for the Treaty – but all because of the final parting in that body which had won the love of Ireland and the respect of the world

Dramatic as the scene was, it was only the end of the beginning. Two days Griffith later defeated De Valera in the election for president of the Dáil (sixty votes to fifty-eight). Griffith's new cabinet contained only two other

Michael Collins

W.T. Cosgrave

survivors of previous cabinets: Collins and W.T. Cosgrave.

While the Dáil vote on the Treaty was significant in terms of what it signalled for the future of Irish republican nationalism, a further step was required to give formal legal effect to the pro-Treaty vote. Under the Better Government of Ireland Act 1920, the assent of the House of Commons of Southern Ireland, a legal fiction created to mirror the parliament established in Belfast at the same time, was required. The Pro-Treaty Sinn Féin TDs saw themselves as constituting this body, having been elected in the May 1921 general election held under the terms of the act. They were joined by four members elected by the voters from Dublin University (Trinity College Dublin). This parliament met once, on Saturday 14 January 1922 in the Mansion House. Following procedure, members also elected a Provisional Government to oversee the transition to a self-governing entity. Collins was elected chairman of the Provisional Government, which contained several members of the Dáil cabinet. For several months afterwards, the twenty-six counties had two administrations governing it.

Sinn Féin, the solid political bloc that had contested the general elections of 1918 and 1921 on a platform of self-determination, was now disintegrating slowly. Nevertheless, it was done in an atmosphere of cordiality, or so the press reported. A meeting of the party's governing Ard Comhairle in the Mansion House on 12 January saw pro-Treaty candidates win most seats on the Standing Committee, which effectively held the levers of party power on a day-to-day basis. The way was now clear for two political organisations, one pro-Treaty and the other anti-Treaty, to contest whatever elections would be called in the coming months.

The first organisation to come out against the Treaty was Cumann na mBan, whose executive voted by 24 votes to 2 to not support 'the Articles of Treaty signed in London'. Members of the organisation picketed the meeting of the House of Commons of Southern Ireland on 14 January. A delegate convention held on 5 February voted (419 votes to 63) to reaffirm 'allegiance to the Republic'. Some of the leading members of the organisation – Jennie Wyse Power, Louise Gavan Duffy (daughter of George Gavan Duffy), Mabel Fitzgerald (wife of Desmond Fitzgerald, Minister for Propaganda in the Dáil government), Min Ryan (wife of Richard Mulcahy), Annie Blythe (wife of Ernest), and Brigid O'Higgins (wife of Kevin) – voted against the motion of allegiance. Other leading members – Máire Comerford, Sheila (Sighle) Humphreys, Countess Markievicz, Mary MacSwiney, and Kate O'Callaghan – voted for the motion. Shortly after the convention, those who had voted against the motion founded Cumann na Saoirse which, unlike Cumann na mBan, did not possess any military side to its activities.

Yet, the major question revolved around an organisation with more power of life and death than any of the totemic political figures who dominated the immediate months after the signing of the Treaty. Tensions within the IRA, already evident before the Treaty vote, now escalated. Republican units of the army in south Tipperary under the command of Denis Lacey, O/C of the Third Tipperary Brigade, raided several military establishments in Clonmel following the withdrawal of British forces from the town. Although this was not an isolated example, there was anxiety among members of the Provisional Government reading about military installations, mostly in the south and west, being handed over to Republican IRA commanders. But a more serious event two weeks after Clonmel brought all sides to the brink of outright fighting.

On 18 February Liam Forde, O/C of the Mid-Limerick IRA Brigade, repudiated the authority of GHQ and occupied the recently vacated barracks in Limerick City. GHQ responded by ordering the closest pro-Treaty IRA unit, Michael Brennan's First Western Division (FWD) in Clare, into Limerick to re-take the barracks. Anti-Treaty troops from Ernie O'Malley's Second Southern Division (SSD) and Liam Lynch's First Southern Division (FSD) raced into Limerick and occupied several hotels and the mental asylum. Others such as Seamus Robinson, Rory O'Connor and Tom Barry also travelled to join in the standoff.

The arrival of these seasoned War of Independence veterans as support to the Republican IRA units already present caused alarm among local politicians and the pro-Treaty GHQ officers. Stephen O'Mara, the mayor of the city, intervened in the standoff and both sides agreed to negotiations. Liam Lynch and Oscar Traynor, O/C Dublin No. 1 IRA Brigade, travelled to Limerick to talk with

Michael Brennan

Liam Lynch

Forde, Robinson, O'Connor and Barry. Ernie O'Malley had members of the SSD march and counter march outside the barracks occupied by Brennan's FWD to give the appearance of large numbers of anti-Treaty troops flooding into the city. By the middle of March, the standoff was over. Brennan's troops ceded control of the barracks to O'Malley and his men; all other troops left the city.

While the Limerick crisis was developing, political events moved swiftly. Delegates at the Sinn Féin Ard Fheis on 22–23 February voted by a majority to accept the Treaty. This meeting was the last united gathering of the movement that had brought about the struggle for independence. During the Ard Fheis De Valera and Griffith met and agreed to postpone the scheduled April elections until the constitution was finalised. Dáil Éireann ratified the Griffith-De Valera agreement on 2 March. That same day Republican IRA volunteers landed a consignment of German-purchased arms and ammunition at Helvick Head, Co. Waterford.

Later in March, anti-Treaty IRA forces in Cork city staged a daring capture of the British Admiralty vessel, the *Upnor*. The vessel was laden with guns and equipment from the British military being transported from Ireland to the Royal Arsenal at Woolwich in London. Plans had been drawn up to capture the ship at sea outside the entrance to Cork Harbour. However, on 29 March the ship sailed unexpectedly. Several Cork City IRA officers, including Dan ('Sandow') O'Donovan and Seán O'Hegarty, eventually commandeered a tug boat, the *Warrior*, and gave chase. At dusk that evening the *Warrior* intercepted the *Upnor*, and an IRA party seized the ship. With the assistance of a Cobh fisherman, the *Upnor* and *Warrior* sailed into Ballycotton at around 10 p.m. Once berthed, a force of some 200 men began unloading the *Upnor*'s cargo, which was completed at 10 a.m. the following morning, 30 March. Overall, some 1500 rifles, 1000 revolvers, 55 Lewis light machine guns, 6 Maxim machine guns, 3 Vickers automatic machine guns, 3,000 hand grenades, and over half a million rounds of ammunition were captured. The raid was a significant coup for the anti-Treaty forces.

Meantime a campaign to convene an IRA convention was gathering pace. Mulcahy had obtained permission from the Dáil cabinet for one to meet on 26 March. However, it was O'Duffy in his role as chief of staff who issued the invitation, and when it became clear that many delegates selected would be anti-Treaty Republican, permission was withdrawn and a proclamation forbidding the gathering was published on 15 March.

Aware that the split in the IRA was deepening, Mulcahy secretly met with Liam Lynch and other FSD officers in Mallow on 20 March. The meeting agreed to avert an open conflict provided an army convention met by 16 April. Mulcahy was condemned by his colleagues for holding such a meeting, and the proposals were rejected.

Two days later many newspapers carried a manifesto summoning the convention to meet in Dublin on 26 March as previously arranged. Rory O'Connor was interviewed also. When asked if a military dictatorship was a possibility, O'Connor replied: 'You can take it that way if you like'. It was, he argued, impossible for him and his men to swear allegiance to any government then in existence. With over fifty senior officers also putting their names to the manifesto (including O'Connor, Liam Mellows, Seán Russell, Lynch, O'Malley and Traynor) a clear split in the IRA was now unavoidable.

On 26 March, 223 Republican IRA delegates convened at the Mansion House. They reaffirmed allegiance to the Republic, approved plans for a new constitution and elected a Republican Army Executive (RAE) to run the army. The gathering met again on 9 April, where the new constitution (drafted by O'Connor, Mellows, Lynch and O'Malley, see appendix) was approved. Among the provisions was an amending of the oath taken by all IRA members (first introduced in 1920) to include supporting and defending the Irish Republic 'against all enemies, foreign and domestic'. At this meeting, many of the more moderate members resigned from the RAE in protest at plans to disrupt planned Dáil elections. The executive was now composed of the hard-line Republicans in the IRA.

Three nights after the convention, battalions of the Dublin Brigade occupied the Four Courts; Kilmainham Gaol was occupied the following day. O'Connor set up RAE headquarters in the former shortly after, and by the end of the month had been joined by Mellows, O'Malley, Seán MacBride and others.

The divisions and leadership vacuum in the IRA throughout April provoked a series of violent outbreaks around the country. Some of these occurrences were responses to the anti-Catholic violence in Northern Ireland. By far the most serious and controversial of these outbreaks started on 26 April and centred on the valley of the Bandon River in west Cork; several people were murdered before local commanders Tom Hales and Barry returned and regained control.

Other violent attacks pointed to a general breakdown in law and order. In Killarney, a platform on which Collins was due to speak on 22 April was burned, but the rally went ahead on the steps of the nearby Franciscan Friary. On the same day Brigadier General George Adamson, a pro-Treaty IRA officer in Athlone, was killed attempting to recover a car commandeered by local Republican IRA forces. Reprisal attacks were also becoming common: Michael Sweeney, a Republican prisoner, was executed by a maverick troop of pro-Treaty IRA forces in Dublin.

Further additions to the casualty list came at the start of May. Republican IRA forces attempted to seize the barracks and other key buildings in Kilkenny. In Dublin, the Four Courts garrison attempted to expand their footprint in the city, and seized two buildings on Essex Quay, the Masonic Hall on Molesworth Street and the famous bastion of southern Irish unionism, the Kildare Street Club.

Peace initiatives in May, at all levels, attempted to avert civil war. These were unsuccessful, but on 20 May Collins and De Valera agreed to conduct an election based on a 'pact'. Sinn Féin would field candidates on a pro-Treaty and anti-Treaty slate. Griffith and other Provisional

Michael Collins making a speech in Clonakilty, Co. Cork, circa April–May 1922.

Government members were annoyed at this plan, as it suggested that Collins was becoming more independent from his pro-Treaty colleagues. Meanwhile, Collins and Griffith were engaged in discussions with Colonial Office officials in London over the proposed constitution of the new Irish state.

By the middle of June the quasi-truce in the IRA was over. Republican IRA units were freely intimidating candidates in Tipperary, Waterford, Kilkenny, Mayo, Kerry, Limerick, Clare, Leitrim, Roscommon and Donegal. Both Cumann na mBan and Cumann na Saoirse had campaigned for the reduction in voting age from 30 to 21, but Griffith refused their pleas because there was insufficient time to update electoral registers. This added another layer of controversy onto an already febrile political landscape.

Arriving back from London on the night of 13 June, Collins left Dublin for Cork the next evening. On his arrival, he gave an impromptu speech where he advised voters:

> vote for the candidates whom [you] … think will best carry on in the future the work that [you] … want carried on … the country must have the representatives that it wants.

On 16 June, pro-Treaty Sinn Féin candidates won fifty-eight of the 128 available seats. Anti-Treaty candidates won thirty-five seats, Labour seventeen seats, Farmers' Party and independent candidates seven seats each, and four were elected by Dublin University. Only two women, Mary MacSwiney and Kate O'Callaghan, both anti-Treaty, were elected.

On 18 June, the RAE met and resolved to break the 1921 truce. Ex-RIC men had been attacked in several locations since the start of June. Four days later Sir Henry Wilson, the British government's military advisor in Northern Ireland was assassinated outside his home in London. Sensing that Dublin Republicans had ordered Wilson's murder, Churchill ordered the remaining British Army units in Dublin to seize the Four Courts. This was superseded by Lloyd George, who gave Collins and Griffith an ultimatum to have O'Connor and his men arrested before military action was launched.

In his position as commander-in-chief of the new National Army, staffed mostly by pro-Treaty IRA volunteers, Collins was placed in an invidious position. The arrest and counter-capture of Republican volunteer Leo Henderson and J.J. 'Ginger' O'Connell only served to hasten the decision. O'Connor and his men were ordered to leave the Four Courts at 3.30 a.m. on the morning of Wednesday 28 June 1922, shortly before sunrise. Field guns and cannons had been stationed on the quays across the River Liffey by National Army troops aided by their British Army counterparts. Forty-five minutes later, these

Kate O'Callaghan and Mary MacSwiney

guns and cannons began firing shells at the building at fifteen-minute intervals.

The battle begins ... Dublin, 1922.

Phase 1

July – December 1922

With the noise of the shells raining on the Four Courts ringing in their ears, Republican IRA leaders met at the Clarence Hotel across the River Liffey. De Valera, Brugha, Lynch, Moylan, Deasy, P.J. Ruttledge and new chief of staff Maurice ('Moss') Twomey attended, along with offiers of the Western Division. The decision to support the Four Courts garrison was swiftly arrived at, after which Lynch, Deasy, Seán Moylan, Con Moylan, Twomey and Seán Culhane set out for Kingsbridge Station to catch a train for Mallow. On their way, they were halted by a squad of National Army troops under the command of Liam Tobin, placed under arrest, and taken to Wellington Barracks on Dublin's South Circular Road. There Eoin O'Duffy questioned them before they were released and allowed continue their journey.

At the Four Courts, the shelling continued for two further days. On 30 June, the building caught fire and spread quickly to adjoining buildings. The Public Record Office, containing thousands of precious documents dating back to 1174, was destroyed in an explosion. O'Connor and the garrison surrendered and were lined up on the quay outside to be marched to Mountjoy Jail. On the way six, including O'Malley, escaped.

An impromptu coalition of Labour Party leader Thomas Johnson, lord mayor of Dublin Laurence O'Neill and the Catholic archbishop of Dublin Edward Byrne twice attempted in the first weeks of fighting to bring about a truce. On both occasions, their overtures were rejected by the Provisional Government, which had determined at a meeting on 1 July 'that the attack on other Irregular [Republican] strongholds should be vigorously continued'. A further attempt by a large delegation of women from across the political divide led by Maud Gonne, Hannah Sheehy-Skeffington, Louie Bennett and Rosamund Jacob to mediate between Traynor and Griffith was rejected by the latter. Mulcahy was given *de facto* command of the National Army, with Collins assuming the portfolio of Minster for Defence while continuing to act as commander-in-chief.

Following their escape from the Four Courts, Dublin Republican IRA members under the command of Oscar Traynor seized several buildings in Sackville Street, Parnell Street, and Capel Street. Other buildings were later taken overlooking Gardiner Street, Lower Abbey Street, and the ruins of the Customs House. Together these streets acted as the boundaries of a cordon in the north inner city. Traynor's headquarters was in 'The Block' on Marlborough Street.

In the defence of this cordon, women played a prominent role. Constance Markievicz acted as a sniper from the roof of a building on Earl Street, Delia Larkin ferried ammunition to snipers on City Quay, and many members of Cumann na mBan (including Máire Comerford, Nora Connolly and her sister Ina) worked as nurses, drivers and messengers. In his memoirs O'Malley expressed his admiration for women practising their driving skills under heavy barrage: '[T]hey practised gear changes up and down streets, and back lanes until they felt themselves sufficiently skilled to act as despatch carriers'. Madge Clifford worked as a secretary to the Four Courts garrison, issuing proclamations and declarations. After the fall of the buildings, she escaped with O'Malley and continued working as his secretary.

Outside Dublin, Republicans mobilised to relieve Traynor. The South Dublin and Mid-Kildare brigades rallied in and around Blessington. O'Malley mobilised several brigades in Tipperary to join them. Together these units were to march on Dublin, their objective being the capture of the Provisional Government's seat in the Royal College of Science on Merrion Street.

These plans failed, because on 2 July the National Army attacked Traynor's positions in and around 'The Block'. Although Republicans fought hard, for example around the Swan public house on York Street, many evacuated south across the Liffey. Those that remained surrendered outside the Hammam Hotel on 5 July. Controversially, Cathal Brugha was shot in the leg at some stage during this surrender; he died two days later. His death came as a shock to many in the Republican leadership, but it was not

Cathal Brugha

the only controversial episode during this period of fighting. National Army officers alleged that Republicans used the Red Cross flag as cover for military operations, including using nursing stations as military posts and having vehicles emblazoned with the Red Cross flag and logo smuggling guns and ammunition out of the city.

From 7 to 10 July 1922 Republicans and National Army units fought across three counties to the south and west of Dublin: Kildare, Wicklow and Wexford. Sporadic fighting broke out in Kilkenny also.

A pause in the fighting followed. At the start of August, Republicans attempted to cut off communications between Dublin and the rest of the country via a series of attacks called 'the night of the Bridges'. These attacks were foiled when a raid in Rathfarnham uncovered the plans. The following night 100 Republican soldiers were captured. Follow-up searches in Wicklow led to fifty-five more arrests. By the end of the month, another 310 Republicans had been captured in the city and county.

Once the initial fighting in Dublin had subsided, the focus on both sides switched to Munster. From July to September 1922, some of the most prolonged fighting of

Barricades in Dublin.

the war took place in the province. National Army forces from Dublin attacked from two directions. Units from Dublin and Kilkenny moved south to Waterford and west through Tipperary. At the other end of the province Brennan's FWD combined with units travelling from Kildare, Leix and King's County to battle for Limerick city before turning south and west towards Cork and Kerry. On the Republican side, Liam Lynch (who had succeeded Moss Twomey as chief of staff) moved GHQ from Dublin to Limerick shortly after his arrival in Mallow.

The battle for Limerick belatedly began on 19 July, following the collapse of a hastily arranged truce 'between Executive [Republican] forces and Beggar's Bush [National Army]'. Despite heavy fighting that held up National Army troops, casualties on both sides were relatively light: eight

National Army soldiers were killed, while Republican deaths numbered between ten and twenty. Liam Lynch escaped to Clonmel, and remaining Republican forces evacuated south and west of the city.

Set piece battles between both sides in Munster were uncommon from this point. Republicans reverted to the trusted guerrilla tactics to stem the flow of the National Army advance deep into the province. Fierce fighting broke out in the weeks after the capture of Limerick in the area of the 'Kilmallock Triangle' (Bruff, Bruree and Kilmallock). National Army intelligence suggested somewhere in the region of 1,500 Republicans had been mobilised to defend this area. After days of combat, the triangle was eventually outflanked from the south-east and north-west, and Republicans evacuated into northern Cork and Kerry.

By far the largest concentration of Republican forces in the country was in west Cork and the south of Kerry. A daring series of seaborne landings at Youghal, Cork harbour, Union Hall, Kenmare and Fenit in the first week of August resulted in disruption to the Republican forces in these areas. In Cork, the villages of Passage West, Monkstown and Douglas saw heavy fighting. Fenit, in the words of National Army officer Niall Harrington, 'could have been our Gallipoli had the Republican leaders appreciated its importance relative to their Munster "front".' This underlined that not all the National Army advances in Munster were as straightforward as appeared. Nevertheless, by the middle of August the Republican

'Munster Republic' had been reduced considerably in area.

On 12 August Griffith died suddenly from a cerebral haemorrhage. Effective control of the Provisional Government passed to Collins, who was also commander-in-chief of the pro-Treaty army. Collins arrived in Cork on 20 August on a mission that remains shrouded in controversy to this day. Shortly after his arrival in the city, he visited several banks that were known to have substantial amounts of money lodged by Republicans on deposit. This money included the proceeds of taxation collected from local businesses in the city under duress. By seizing these assets, Collins hoped to drain the lifeblood from the Munster Republic and hasten the end of the war.

However, on the day of Collins' arrival in Cork a high-

Arthur Griffith's funeral.

level Republican meeting at Ballyvourney, while agreeing to open negotiation channels, decided to put Liam Lynch's Operating Order No. 19 into action, forming flying columns and engaging National Army troops in a guerrilla war. Far from ending the war, Collins' presence in Cork was a signal to increase the intensity of the struggle. A general National Army report on 22 August concurred: 'Our forces have captured towns, but they have not captured Irregulars [Republicans] and arms on anything like a large scale, and, until this is done, the Irregulars will be capable of guerrilla warfare.'

On the same day that report was produced, Collins undertook a tour of National Army positions in west and south-west Cork. Again, it is a matter of continuous debate and conjecture as to his motivation for this tour. Emmet Dalton, the mastermind behind the sea landings earlier in the month and the National Army commander in Cork, accompanied him on this tour, which fell prey to one of the first enactments of Lynch's Order No. 19 near the small hamlet of Beal na Bláth a few miles south-west of Crookstown. Engaging the small firing party that held up his convoy, Collins was shot in the head and killed instantly.

The tragic nature of his tour had an element of farce in the twenty-mile journey the convoy endured back to Cork City: wrong turnings, diversions across fields, shots fired at priests unwilling to administer the last rites to the corpse of the National Army commander-in-chief, all formed beads on the *Via Dolorosa* of the Provisional Government forces. Collins' body was borne aboard the SS *Classic*, landing at Dun Laoghaire on Wednesday 23 August. Following a ceremonial lying-in-state and a funeral mass in Dublin's pro-cathedral on Monday 28 August, he was buried with full military honours in Glasnevin Cemetery.

In the space of less than two weeks, the fledgling government tasked with fighting the Civil War had lost its two most prominent figures. Mulcahy moved quickly to prevent disorder among the army ranks and quelled any potential reprisals planned to avenge Collins. He wrote to all members of the army: 'Let no act of cruel reprisal blemish your bright honour … To you falls his [Collins'] unfinished work. No darkness in the hour; no loss of comrades will daunt you at it. Ireland: the Army serves – strengthened by its sorrow.'

Dublin and Munster were the central theatres of the Civil War, but not the only ones. Forgotten for several decades were the conflicts in Connacht and Ulster. The National Army occupied Galway city shortly after the fall of the Four Courts, but for much of July fighting raged on the outskirts of the city and in Kilchreest, Gort, Ballinasloe and Carnmore. But one of the first serious outrages in the province happened on 30 June, when Republicans attacked Clifden and burned an orphanage, where twenty-five boys and staff lived. Most if not all were Protestant. Speaking in the House of Commons Sir Edward Carson referred to the burning as 'one of the very worst [cases] of the many hundreds that had been sent to him within the past two months.'

Much of the fighting in Connacht had an element of continuity from the War of Independence and the desire to accompany a political revolution with a parallel transformation of the class structure. The echoes of the land wars of 1879–81, 1886–91 and 1898–1907 resurfaced in 1919–21 and continued through the Civil War. During the war seventeen 'big houses' in the county were burned, placing Galway third on the list behind Tipperary (twenty-nine) and Cork (nineteen). In this, Liam Mellows and his followers were hugely influential. His article in the *Workers' Republic*, the newspaper of the Communist Party of Ireland, on 22 July 1922 in which he lambasted the labour movement, encapsulated his thinking. The struggle for an Irish Republic, he wrote, had a triple significance: political, intellectual and economic. By fighting for an Irish Republic people were fighting to get rid of an economic system 'that had its roots in foreign domination'.

While social revolution was foremost in the minds of many Republicans in Galway, their counterparts in Mayo combined this with probably the most fervent defence of the Republic outside of Munster. Early in the year, Republicans had occupied the former RIC barracks in Ballinrobe, Claremorris, Castlebar, Ballina and Swinford. The war in the county commenced on 29 June with an ambush near Bohola (halfway between Castlebar and Swinford), during which Republican Capt. William Moran and National Army soldier Tom Ruane were killed.

National Army troops from Sligo and Athlone conducted sweeps in the county against the IRA, initially focusing on the Ox Mountains but later in the western and southern regions. On 24 July, Brig.-Gen. Joe Ring landed detachments of National Army troops at Westport. These troops moved quickly eastward and northward, capturing the barracks in Castlebar and Ballina the following day. Newport became a centre of heavy fighting for a few weeks in July and August, before being evacuated by the National Army at the end of September. From August until October 1922 National Army and IRA units in Mayo fought each other on a regular basis.

In Sligo and Roscommon, Republicans were better organised than their National Army counterparts, and for much of 1922 held the upper hand in both counties. Yet, the force of numbers tilted the war in the National Army's favour as time went on. The most controversial episode of the war in both counties came in September, when six major Republican figures, including Brian MacNeill (son of Provisional Government minister Eoin), were killed in an encounter on Benbulben mountain. Their funerals drew huge numbers onto the streets of Sligo town, and in the opinion of Moss Twomey dealt 'a very severe blow to the Brigade which had practically to be reorganised again'. Yet, the IRA survived in both counties because of a morass of issues within the National Army – poor morale, organisational issues, and shortages of supplies and equipment all contributed towards a lack of momentum.

Neighbouring Donegal experienced the Civil War in a different manner. With the creation of the Northern Ireland state in July 1921, the IRA faced a challenge from the new state's police force, the B Specials. On 22 May 1922, Craig's government declared Sinn Féin and the IRA illegal. The following week Specials occupied the village of Pettigo and surrounding countryside in Donegal. This began a standoff with the IRA and the National Army which lasted beyond the Civil War.

Yet the IRA in Northern Ireland were, for the first three months of the war, supported by Collins before his death. A boycott of Belfast goods that had begun in late 1921 continued and accelerated as 1922 wore on. On 3 June, the Provisional Government had resolved to continue a policy of 'peaceful obstruction ... towards the Belfast Government' but forbade National Army troops from crossing the border.

While this did not completely eradicate attacks by forces linked to Collins and the government – such as at Altnaveigh, Co. Armagh on 17 June, when six loyalists were shot dead by men in police uniforms later described as 'southern terrorists'– the splintering of the IRA in the counties bordering the new Northern Ireland state reduced the frequency of raids and attacks. The civil war in Ulster became less of a nationalist-unionist death fight and more of a struggle for control of militant nationalism.

Many Republicans in Donegal at the outbreak of the war were from Munster, Tyrone or Derry. Shortly after the Four Courts attack, National Army troops seized the strategic locations of Finner Camp, Ballyshannon and Buncrana. Republicans retreated to Raphoe, while the flying columns of the No. 1 and No. 2 Brigades were captured. Negotiations between Republican leader Charlie Daly and Joe Sweeney (commander of the National Army forces in the county) for a truce broke down quickly, and plans were laid for a rapid National Army sweep of the county. Morale among Republican forces dropped sharply as they watched their comrades in other areas engage the National Army. A decision to evacuate the county of Republicans was postponed on several occasions before, in November 1922, Ernie O'Malley (by this stage in command of Republican forces in the midlands, north and west) ordered Seán Lehane, who succeeded Daly in overall command of the Donegal IRA, to leave the county.

The best-equipped and organised Republican force in Northern Command (which covered Ulster plus the northern half of Co. Louth) was Frank Aiken's Fourth Northern Division, covering most of Armagh, west Down and north Louth. A native of Armagh, Aiken held neutral from the splits in Sinn Féin and the IRA in early 1922, preferring to concentrate on resolving the Northern Ireland situation. Many under his command did not and refused to support the Provisional Government.

On 16 July, National Army troops seized Aiken's HQ and garrison in Dundalk and placed him and over 200 of his men under arrest in the barracks. Twelve days later, he led a spectacular escape, following the mining of barrack walls. Ernie

Ernie O'Malley

O'Malley sent Todd Andrews to Louth to find out Aiken's precise position on the Treaty. Though he refused to give Andrews a definitive answer, Aiken allowed him to participate in the audacious recapture of the town on 14 August.

Cardinal Michael Logue's may have influenced his eventual adherence to the Republican side with his letter of 30 July, where he angrily denounced the actions of 'desperate rascals and robbers ... They are bringing a respectable Catholic town into disgrace'. However, Aiken's and his unit's hold on the town was tenuous; National Army troops from the Fifth Northern Division recaptured the town two days later. Aiken's subsequent efforts during the civil war turned out to be less military and more political. O'Malley wrote to Liam Lynch in September that Aiken's policy of non-intervention was 'mistaken'. In October Aiken was elected to the IRA Executive, and succeeded Liam Lynch as chief-of-staff in April 1923. Many IRA members in Northern Ireland felt betrayed by the failure of the policies carried out since the creation of the statelet. National Army forces, particularly after August 1922 and perhaps because of the deaths of Collins and Griffith, focused almost exclusively on securing the twenty-six counties from Republican attack. Even on the Republican side, a coherent policy towards Northern Ireland never existed outside of Aiken's own division. Kevin O'Shiel, a native of Omagh in Co. Tyrone and Michael Collins' adviser on affairs in Northern Ireland, who later served as assistant legal adviser to the Provisional Government, reflected that Republicans had 'tacitly agreed to leave the Six Counties alone until the findings of the [Boundary] Commission'.

Seán Mac Eoin

Elsewhere guerrilla fighting and small-scale engagements highlighted the first phase of the Civil War. Much of this fighting took place in the counties around Athlone, which housed the National Army's Western Command headed by Longford native Seán MacEoin. In lieu of a proper police force, troops under MacEoin's command fought a battle over law and order rather than full-scale attacks on IRA units. Shortage of manpower at leadership level hampered the Republican effort in the region.

Both sides, in fact, were over-stretched. MacEoin's command was the largest in the National Army's command structure, running from Sligo in the north to Clare in the south and taking in most of Westmeath, Longford and western Cavan. On the Republican side, there was less strategic command than in the National Army, although O'Malley did attempt to rectify this when given command of the region. Much of the operational work fell on local leaders.

The early months of the war saw MacEoin's forces attempting to clear Republicans from the major towns in the region. When the new Curragh Command was created shortly before Collins' death, it theoretically relieved some of the pressure on MacEoin. However, this command took time and resources to operate effectively. At Custume Barracks in Athlone, there were 720 troops, 249 rifles, 100 grenades and eighty-seven revolvers; the picture was similar at barracks in Sligo, Birr and Roscommon.

In September, the Provisional Government enacted two policies aimed at curbing the influence of Republicans. O'Higgins told Mulcahy that, now the major urban centres were in the hands of the National Army, the war was now 'more a question of armed crime'. Therefore, the new police force, the Civic Guard, was inaugurated under the command of Michael Staines. A significant aspect of this new force was that it was unarmed. Later in the month the new Dáil, with a supplementary Army Emergency Powers Resolution (AEPR) enacted, passed public safety legislation.

Under this new legislation, Republicans captured by National Army forces were denied prisoner-of-war status and were deemed to be in rebellion against the lawful government; they were further denied the right of *habeas corpus*. The government offered an amnesty to IRA volunteers to surrender before 15 October, and a pastoral letter from Catholic bishops issued on 10 October condemned those continuing to fight against the government and excommunicated those still engaged in the fight after the amnesty deadline had passed.

In the background work on a constitution for the new Irish Free State continued under the leadership of Hugh

Kennedy. On the Republican side an IRA Army Executive meeting in Tipperary on 16–17 October agreed to the formation of a new 'government of the republic', based on the thirty-five anti-Treaty TDs elected the previous June. A meeting of those TDs, not in jail, took place the following week in Dublin.

There, De Valera was elected president, and a twelve-member cabinet or 'council of state' was selected to govern 'until such time as the elected Parliament of the Republic [could] … freely assemble'. This government proclaimed themselves the true heirs of the founding fathers of 1916 and 1919. Although they never formally met, the symbolism was important, as De Valera admitted to Joseph McGarrity in America: he 'did not care what [sort of] Republican government [was] … set up so long as some one [was]'.

On 6 December 1922, one year exactly from the signing of the Treaty, the Irish Free State formally came into existence. Its founding was overshadowed by events in the war, but the provisional nature of Cosgrave's government was gone. He and his colleagues now formally controlled the machinery of government of an Irish state and were determined to exercise them. Paradoxically the creation of the Free State was a boon to Republicans also; they could now point to the real differences between what they were fighting for and what had been established.

DECEMBER 1922 – MAY 1923

The latter half of the Civil War period saw direct engagements between National Army (or 'Free State') forces and Republicans decrease, and violent killings on either side increase. Both sides used all means at their disposal to solidify their positions. Attempts at peace talks were made, particularly during February 1923, but the waves of killings did not stop until Frank Aiken, then IRA chief-of-staff, issued a 'dump arms' order in May. Even then, it is arguable that the war did not end for some years, and the war by guns became a war by words for several generations.

On 7 December 1922 Seán Hales TD was assassinated outside the Ormonde Hotel in Dublin; his companion Pádraic Ó Máille was seriously injured in the shooting. In retaliation, four prominent Republicans were executed the following morning in Mountjoy Jail (see next chapter). Republicans in Dublin, upset and outraged at the killings of comrades, targeted the houses of prominent 'Free State' TDs and government officials.

Three nights later, the houses of Seán McGarry (TD and IRB member) in Fairview and Michael McDunphy (assistant secretary to the government) in nearby Clonliffe were set ablaze. The homes of Postmaster-General J.J. Walsh on Blessington Street and Cumann na Saoirse leader Jennie Wyse Power on Earlsfort Terrace were also targeted. Two nights later attacks were carried out on the home of Lord Glenavy in Kimmage and state solicitor and Sinn Féin supporter William Corrigan on Dame Street. Shots were fired at Mulcahy on the same night. Later in the month, Denis McCullough (former IRB president and a key figure in the renewal of the brotherhood at the turn of the twentieth century) saw his shop in Dawson Street destroyed following an explosion. Later in the month Seamus Dwyer, a former TD who voted for the Treaty but did not stand in the 'pact' election, was shot dead in his shop in Rathmines.

In January, the attacks in Dublin continued. The homes of state solicitor M.A. Corrigan, John Arnott (chairman of the *Irish Times*) and the manager of the *Irish Independent* were burned. Members of the new Irish Free State senate were also targeted. These included the heir to the Marquis of Lansdowne, the chairman of Bank of Ireland, the former commander of British forces in Ireland, Sir Horace Plunkett (founder of the cooperative movement), and members of the Guinness family. As many of these were also Protestant unionists, there was a tinge of sectarianism added to the anti-capitalism characterising the attacks. Máire Comerford was involved in a plot to kidnap Cosgrave, but these plans were accidentally foiled by Min Ryan, who reported Comerford. She was subsequently arrested and placed in Mountjoy Jail.

Although Republicans did not kill any senator, several were abducted, including John Bagwell, taken from his home near Howth in February and held until the government threatened to execute several Republican prisoners. Also, in February several revenue offices were raided in the Dublin city centre. These attacks were to be accompanied by a wave of assassinations. Frank Henderson, commander of the Dublin IRA, later recalled that he had the opportunity to kill ministers Eamonn Duggan, Fionán Lynch and Seán McGarry but was reluctant to give the order. An attempt to kill Joe McGrath foundered when putative assassins burst into his office on Lord Edward Street only to find it empty! Nevertheless, because of these incidents TDs were billeted in Buswells Hotel and escorted to the Dáil by armed guard.

Unrest, as we have seen, was common in National Army ranks. Yet, in Republican circles internal conflict was also common. One such example came in east Munster and south Leinster (south Tipperary, Waterford and Kilkenny). The Republican situation in south Tipperary remained unchanged from July, when local officers refused to accept orders from nominal superiors. This clash of personalities and objectives was somewhat quelled when Liam Lynch talked of placing Tom Barry in charge of Republican operations in the region. In the National Army camp, indiscipline was becoming a hallmark of activities in some parts of the region, especially in the towns of Clonmel and Callan. In the former town charges of drunkenness among the soldiers were frequent; in the latter a priest told W.T. Cosgrave that National Army members were 'traitorous or semi-mutinous'. Despite not being in theoretical charge of Republican operations in the region, Barry led a group of Cork and Tipperary men in the capture of Carrick-on-Suir on 13 December 1922. Over the following days National Army garrisons in Callan, Thomastown and Mullinavat surrendered to Republican forces, some of whom were dressed in National Army uniforms! An investigation carried out by Comdt-Gen. Eamon Price into the National Army structures of command in the region found that many officers were lax in their duties, despite the shortages of arms and transport. The sub-standard nature of intelligence gathering, Price wrote, was 'indicative of the dry rot which has stolen in here', especially compared with the 'eminently superior' intelligence gathered by the 'Irregulars'. He concluded that a thorough re-organisation of National Army structures in the region was an urgent necessity.

With the onset of winter, the guerrilla war began to peter out in many areas of Munster. Cork, for so long the cockpit of fighting, now saw peace talks occurring. Liam Deasy's arrest on 18 January left a huge void in the Republican leadership in the county, as did Liam Lynch's decision to move three other key leaders – Seán Moylan, Mick Leahy and Pa Murray – to leadership roles in America and Britain. What action occurred was minor and confined to isolated localities near Macroom and Bantry.

In south Tipperary and Waterford, the war waged by

Republicans was neutralised by National Army troops under a new command, though house burnings and uncoordinated attacks on individuals still occurred. In February came the final acts of the war in the area: Dinny Lacey was killed; National Army troops swept through the Glen of Aherlow, the Galtee Mountains and Ballingarry; and Con Moloney was captured along with several colleagues at Rossadrehid at the foot of the Galtees. IRA troops gradually broke into progressively smaller units whose main task was to avoid arrest. In north Tipperary and Limerick IRA units had dissolved into playing minor harassment roles; key leaders such as Paddy Ryan Lacken and Seán Gaynor were arrested, and the final outposts of resistance in the Silvermines Mountains were broken up in March.

Through the winter and spring of 1923, frequent skirmishes and battles raged between the National Army and the IRA in Mayo. Attacks near Kiltimagh and Westport, as well as the on-going battles around Newport, led to several casualties and scores of arrests. A final outburst of activity in April saw IRA deaths in Ballina and in Headford, Co. Galway. On 24 May, the same day as Aiken's 'dump arms' order, National Army forces arrested many of the senior staff of the IRAs Fourth Western Division. This however did not end the violence in Mayo. In June Joe Healy, an IRA volunteer from Ardnaree, was killed near Ballina. Occasional outbursts continued in isolated parts of the county until Christmas.

Sligo IRA units conducted a wave of killings of suspected 'spies and informers' in the Tubbercurry area throughout November 1922. People flocked to the local army barracks in Ballymote and Tubbercurry seeking protection. At the start of 1923, Republicans in Sligo town captured a National Army post near the town hall, and seized twenty-one rifles, four revolvers and 1,300 rounds of ammunition. A few days later, the railway station was destroyed in a spectacular series of explosions.

Although Republicans in the county now held a large arsenal of weapons, thanks in part to the *Upnor* capture, their ability to use them was curtailed by a reorganisation of the National Army. Sweeps and arrests of Republicans rose. A feature of these sweeps was the tit-for-tat house burning: National Army troops burned the houses of two Republicans, while Republicans burned the houses of six families who had members in the National Army.

In the midlands, Republicans resumed attacks on the railway network in and around Athlone early in 1923. By this stage, the almost-constant conflict in and around the town had taken a heavy physical and psychological toll. Athlone Urban District Council teetered on the verge of bankruptcy due to spiralling costs and drastically reduced incomes. Some of the streets in the town were compared with the trenches of Flanders in the First World War. Employment suffered too. In March, Athlone Sawmills closed with the loss of 100 jobs. Much of the blame for this was pointed at the National Army for exporting contracts outside the region. Tramps or 'knights of the road' were a common sight within the town boundaries.

The guerrilla campaigns waged by Republicans scarcely lessened after the Fahereen incident when twenty-seven members of an IRA column from Fahereen near Moate agreed to surrender their arms, claiming they did so under the terms of Liam Deasy's call for surrender in February 1923 (see below pp. 55–56). But this was repudiated by the anti-Treaty press, which carried reports that the Fahereen column surrendered after their O/C David Daly had resigned on health grounds. Members of the column were subsequently involved in an attack on Athlone on 27 February 1923. The Westmeath county coroner reported that his annual total of inquests had been reached in just five or six days, as the county's total of Civil War dead outstripped the total recorded for the War of Independence. By this stage in the war, many confrontations in the region were confined to Saturday nights.

Three major Republican cells had been identified by MacEoin and his men: Kiltoom (headed by Michael Pender), Brideswell and Ballymore on the Athlone to Mullingar road. Many cell members were escapees from Custume Barracks. Operations designed to break up the cells were unsuccessful, mainly, in MacEoin's, opinion because of the support offered to Republicans. Particular attention was paid in National Army reports to the influence 'of the female element' in maintaining this support. Women, it was claimed, were more likely to support the Republicans than the National Army or the Free State government.

Most Republican activity in Longford came after Christmas 1922. MacEoin's preoccupations with his new post as head of the National Army's Western Command led him and his subordinates in Athlone to mostly overlook his native county. Much of the activity in Longford was more akin to civil disobedience and low-level criminality than orchestrated attacks on National Army military posts or barracks. The local press reported mail robberies, post office raids and road blockings in the first few months of 1923. On 26 February Castle Forbes, the seat of the Earl of Granard near Newtown-Forbes, was attacked with two land mines. Although one failed to explode, the other caused extensive damage to the house and adjoining buildings. This attack coincided with, or came shortly after, the attacks on houses of Irish Free State senators in Dublin (Granard was a senator until 1934).

With Liam Deasy's arrest, an opportunity for peace arose. A letter signed by him was sent to all IRA commanders urging them to cease the fighting. Many who read the letter, including Liam Lynch, thought it was a forgery. Ernie O'Malley, who briefly shared a cell with Deasy in Mountjoy, later claimed it took all his self-restraint not to attack him. Frank Carty in Sligo attacked the letter as 'a shameful and cowardly surrender of the Republic whose ultimate victory is assured'.

The 'Deasy Manifesto', as Tom Barry christened it, had a strong effect on the Republican prisoners.

Liam Deasy

55

Some prisoners in Cork jail signed a similar letter to avoid execution. Free State authorities also granted IRA members an amnesty for two weeks in February 1923 to give up arms.

Florence O'Donoghue who, along with Seán O'Hegarty, founded the Neutral IRA in December 1922, superseded Deasy's efforts. O'Donoghue later claimed a membership of 20,000, many of whom were former (i.e., pre-truce) IRA members. Although their attitude towards the Treaty was firmly Republican, the Neutral IRA called for a month-long truce and a conference to settle the war.

While the Neutral IRA was ultimately a failure, and wound up in March 1923, its very existence served as a signal for fresh peace proposals. Dr John Harty, the archbishop of Cashel, assisted by Fr Tom Duggan (a close friend of Tom Barry), produced a document that called for a fresh general election. Before that election, all Republican arms would be dumped by local battalion commanders; after the election all these arms would be handed over to the government.

The IRA First Southern Division debated Dr Harty's proposals on 10 February. Following that meeting Barry, Tom Crofts and Fr Duggan travelled to Dublin to present the proposals to Liam Lynch and call for a meeting of the Army Executive. Lynch was not convinced, and upbraided Barry and Crofts for acting against stated policy. This angered Barry, who verbally assailed Lynch: 'I did more fighting in one week than you did in your whole life'.

A stand-off existed for several weeks during February

and March 1923 between Barry and Crofts on one side and Lynch on the other. Lynch attempted to stall acceptance of the Duggan proposals pending a successful outcome of the so-called 'Jetter business'. Since the start of the year, J.T. ('Jetter') Ryan was active in the USA and Germany attempting to purchase arms and artillery that could be use in mountainous areas. However, correspondence between Ryan and IRA GHQ was intercepted and the purchase plans collapsed.

On 24 March, an IRA Executive meeting began in the Nire valley in Waterford; it took four days to complete because of constant sweeps by Free State forces, which necessitated frequent changes of location. At the meeting, a motion by Barry and Crofts stating that further fighting would 'not further the cause of Independence of the country' was narrowly defeated (six votes to five), which showed the extent to which the peace moves had affected thinking. Austin Stack was captured on 14 April near Ballymacarbery, Co. Waterford and in his possession were letters accepting Dr Harty's peace terms.

Although Dr Harty's peace moves did not ultimately result in a cessation of the fighting, they did show the extent to which Republicans were divided. Lynch's death on 10 April during a fight in the Knockmealdown Mountains near Newcastle, Co. Tipperary, removed the last major barrier in the IRA leadership to peace.

A controversial and confusing episode concerned the visit of Monsignor Luzio, sent apparently at the behest of Pope Pius XI to settle the war, in April 1923. Luzio's visit annoyed Cosgrave and his ministers. He was seen as sympathetic to the Republicans, and as a result was shunned by the government until he was recalled on 25 April. No formal peace talks were held following Aiken's 'dump arms' order on 24 May 1923. Many areas, especially along the western seaboard, grudgingly accepted the order but never fully surrendered.

When did the Civil War formally end? Repercussions of the fighting continued for several years. The anti-Treaty coalition under the Sinn Féin umbrella split again in 1925, when De Valera left to found Fianna Fáil a year later. Tensions continued to splinter the IRA well into the 1930s and 1940s. Likewise, the political and military coalitions on the Free State side were riven with fractures well into the 1930s, until the founding of Fine Gael in 1933. The death of Kevin O'Higgins in August 1927 can be seen as the final casualty of the war.

Kevin O'Higgins

Controversy, Reprisal and Execution during the Civil War

As is so often the case in civil wars, controversy over the conduct of both sides figured heavily. Events in late 1922 and early 1923 created a legacy of bitterness and poisoned relations between Republicans and 'Free Staters' for several generations. The most enduring of these controversies surrounded a policy of summary executions carried out by the Provisional Government from November 1922. And at local level, the conduct of several sections of the National Army also left bitter legacies.

For all the Provisional Governments' successes in the early months of the war, discipline within the ranks of the National Army continued to trouble both GHQ and several ministers. Collins reported shortly after the seizure of the Four Courts that there was 'no army ... only an armed mob'. Many battalions of the National Army were not suitably trained to a sufficiently high level to meet the challenges that a prolonged guerrilla war, mostly against former comrades, posed. Drunkenness and low-level criminality were the major incidents of ill-discipline reported by officers.

Towards the end of 1922 waves of 'dishonourable' killings swept through Dublin. In July, Lynch had issued ordered forbidding the killing of unarmed, surrendered or off-duty National Army soldiers, or using 'dum-dum' bullets (bullets with soft tips which exploded on impact, causing more damage to the body than a conventional bullet). On the pro-Treaty side, Collins had exercised a firm restraining hand for the most part, but his death in August removed this, and his successors in army command and the Provisional Government struggled to restrain those seeking to avenge their dead commander-in-chief.

From the Truce, an *ad hoc* police force under the command of Liam Tobin operated from Oriel House on Westland Row. This group were mostly composed of former members of Collins's Squad and did not come under control of the Provisional Government until shortly after the attack on the Four Courts in June 1922. In August 1922 this group were reorganised: Tobin was placed in charge of a military intelligence section and moved his base to Wellington Barracks; Frank Saurin, a veteran IRA intelligence officer, was appointed o/c of the remainder of this group, which was renamed the Criminal Investigation Department (CID).

By September over 100 men were involved with CID and Oriel House had garnered a fearsome reputation for interrogating and interning suspects. Thomas Derrig, a member of the IRA Army Council, lost 45% of the vision in his left eye having been shot during his arrest in April 1923. Other Republicans captured and brought to Oriel House during the war later testified to being tortured with scissors, pliers, razors and even hot irons. Republicans attempted on two occasions to kill members of the CID. On 17 October

Detective Tony Deane was shot answering the front door of Oriel House. Two weeks later an abortive attempt was made to blow up the building, but only a handful of casualties were reported. In retaliation for Deane's killing, a firefight broke out on nearby Mount Street and Patrick Mannion, an IRA volunteer who had been shot in the leg, was brutally executed via multiple direct gunshots to the head. An inquest into Mannion's death returned a verdict of 'wilful murder'.

On 7 October, three members of Fianna Éireann, the youth wing of the Republican movement, were arrested in Drumcondra. They were taken to Wellington Barracks and interrogated about their activities, which appeared to be little more than propaganda exercises. What happened after their interrogation remains a source of controversy, but the following day their bodies were discovered in a quarry near Clondalkin, close to the Red Cow townland. One body was found to have sixteen bullets in it.

The 'Red Cow killings' set off a wave of revulsion. Pro-Treaty newspapers such as the *Freeman's Journal* and the *Irish Independent* lamented the 'demoralisation of the nation', but also called for the perpetrators to be brought to justice. The inquest into the deaths descended into farce as National Army personnel refused to volunteer information regarding the questioning of the boys. Tim Healy, the razor-tongued ex-Irish Party MP who acted as a legal counsel for the chief suspect Charlie Dalton (brother of Emmet) asked rhetorically if any side could 'set a boundary to the march of extermination?' Despite this charged statement which was widely reported inside and outside Ireland the jury ruled that the boys had been 'killed by gunshots fired by persons unknown'.

In November 1922 Michael Carolan, the Republican IRA Director of Intelligence, produced a list of twelve men who he alleged were members of a 'Free State Murder Gang'. Seven of the twelve names were members of CID, Free State Military Intelligence, or former members of the Squad, including Charlie Dalton. Todd Andrews alleged that 'real or suspected' Republicans were arrested and murdered without recourse to questioning or investigation by Oriel House.

Before his death, Collins had attempted to instil some formal army structures, which included a structure devoted to dealing with disciplinary issues. Cahir Davitt, son of the legendary Michael Davitt, became the new Judge Advocate General (JAG) of the National Army. Davitt's appointment, part of an overall strategy to re- define the army's role within a new Irish state, sparked unease among some of Collins' closest colleagues within GHQ. Gearóid O'Sullivan, the adjutant-general of the National Army, engaged in several acrimonious arguments with Davitt over the conduct of men under his command. Rightly or wrongly, Davitt was seen as interfering with a system of justice which had taken hold during the War of Independence, where IRA units would carry out judgements delivered by the Dáil Courts. While there are no suggestions that this conflict contributed to the continuing ill-discipline, an undercurrent of dissent remained.

This undercurrent surfaced on several occasions after Collins' death. Moral plummeted within the National Army ranks, only exacerbated by the increasing intensity of guerrilla attacks in certain regions of the country. Revenge and retribution attacks on Republican prisoners became all too common. In the autumn of 1922, prisoners in Kerry, Sligo, Cork, Limerick, Tipperary and Mayo were killed. One such case concerned Timothy Kennefick from Coachford, Co. Cork, who was captured during a National Army sweep in the late summer. Kennefick was tortured and savagely beaten before being shot in the head; his body was dumped in a ditch near Macroom. Another target of a revenge killing was Jerry Buckley, who was alleged to have detonated a mine near Macroom, killing six National Army soldiers and mortally wounding Comdt Tom Keogh (a long-standing member of Collins' Squad during the War of Independence). Former members of the Squad in the National Army tracked down Buckley, shot him and dumped his body in the crater left by the explosion.

One of the more egregious of these killings was seventeen-year-old Bartholomew Murphy from Castle-island, Co. Kerry. The National Army, following a failed ambush at Brennan's Glen between Killarney and Farran-fore, captured Murphy. He was taken to a makeshift barracks at the Great Southern Hotel in Killarney, where for some days he was set to work clearing barricades near the town. A few nights later, a second ambush at Brennan's Glen led to three National Army soldiers being killed. That night, Murphy was assaulted and shot dead in the barracks.

At his inquest, the following day Brig.-Gen. Paddy O'Daly told his family that Murphy had been killed while being transported from Brennan's Glen to Killarney and asserted: 'under no circumstances do we permit our political prisoners to be ill-treated'.

Murphy's killing, along with those of Jack Galvin from Killorglin and two others from Tralee the previous month, again placed pressure on Richard Mulcahy and W.T. Cosgrave. The enactment of a Public Safety Bill in September 1922 was followed by the Army Emergency Powers Resolution (AEPR). The AEPR established military courts with power to punish 'persons found guilty of acts calculated to interfere with or delay the effective establishment of the authority of the government'. These acts included: possessing 'without proper authority' fire-arms, ammunition or explosives; arson, looting, or the destruction of property; taking part in or aiding attacks on National Army troops; or breaching any orders or regulations made by the Army Council. Anyone found guilty of contravening the AEPR was to be punished with 'severe penalties', including death. Captured Republicans were denied prisoner-of-war status and were deemed to be in rebellion against the government. They were further denied the right of *habeas corpus*. The resolutions' legality was debated by contemporaries and has been the subject of controversy ever since. Speaking in the Dáil Mulcahy defended the introduction of the measure: 'Life must be taken if necessary and it is the responsibility of the government to say that it must be taken'.

The first life to be taken following the passage of the AEPR was the unauthorised execution of Jack Lawlor in Ballyheigue, Co. Kerry. However, the execution of James Fisher, John Gaffney, Richard Twohig and Peter Cassidy by firing squad at Wellington Barracks, Dublin, on 17 November marked the formal start of the execution policy. Lawlor had been killed following a botched mission to recover firearms from a local graveyard; the four executed in Dublin had been found in possession of various armaments, contravening the terms of the AEPR.

Less than a week after the executions at Wellington Barracks, Erskine Childers was shot by firing squad at Beggars Bush Barracks. Recent research has established that Collins had ordered Childers' arrest before his death, but Childers had managed to evade capture. On the morning of 10 November, he was arrested at the home of his cousin Robert Barton in Co. Wicklow, having brandished a revolver at the party of National Army troops sent to arrest him. After his arrest Childers was brought to Portobello Barracks where he was beaten and kicked so severely that he was unable to lie down. His trial was lengthy, given his status within the Republican movement and a subsequent appeal based on the right of *habeas corpus*. Yet the appeal was dismissed on the evening of 23 November 1922; less than twelve hours later Childers was executed. Childers' execution was, in the words of De Valera, a 'big blow'. Some of his former colleagues, including George Gavan Duffy, decried the swiftness and secrecy surrounding his arrest, trial and execution. Childers himself in his final hours wrote to his wife that he hoped his death 'would somehow – I know not how – save the lives of others – arrest this policy of executions.'

Childers' death brought a quick response from Liam Lynch. On 30 November, IRA members received orders to kill any TD who had voted to introduce the AEPR. This did little to halt the immediate rush to execution. Eight more Republicans, four each in Kerry and Dublin, were sentenced to death. The Kerry prisoners' sentences were delayed while legal argument raged. In Dublin, three of the four were executed; the sole survivor, Joseph Mallin, seems to have survived because he was the son of a 1916 martyr. Conduct of the war now resembled a vendetta on a national scale.

On 6 December 1922, the Irish Free State came into existence, and Cosgrave was named president of the Executive Council. The following day Seán Hales and Pádraic Ó Máille, two pro-Treaty TDs, were shot at point-blank range outside the Ormonde Hotel on Dublin's

Seán Hales (left)

Pádraic Ó Máille

north quays. Hales died almost instantly, while Ó Máille (the leas-cheann comhairle of the Dáil) survived. Reports of the shooting quickly reached the Dáil; some TDs even left the capital in haste before being returned by the secret service. Hurried meetings of the Executive Council and Army Council took place that evening. Kevin O'Higgins, Minister for Home Affairs, and the man depicted by the press as the defiant face of the new administration, was reluctant to go along with the decision reached by his colleagues. Mulcahy had proposed that the four most senior Republicans then in custody – Liam Mellows, Dick Barrett, Rory O'Connor and Joe McKelvey – would be executed immediately, and Cosgrave agreed.

A memorial poster for Rory O'Connor, Dick Barrett, Liam Mellows and Joseph McKelvey executed on 8 December 1922.

Early in the following morning (8 December 1922), the four men were taken from their cells in Mountjoy Prison, taken outside into the exercise yard and shot by firing squad. Eyewitness accounts told of McKelvey defiant stance, asking to be shot a second and then a third time. Some women prisoners later recounted hearing as many as nine shots following the initial volley.

Shock and outrage greeted the news of the executions. In the Dáil Thomas Johnson, leader of the Labour Party and the opposition, accused the government of killing 'the new state at its birth'. Gavan Duffy likened the executions to a mafia vendetta. The main thrust of the debate inside and outside parliament was to what extent had the government acted outside both the new Free State Constitution and the terms of international law (which allowed for 'belligerent reprisals' against opponents who departed from the accepted standards of war, but said nothing at the time regarding executing prisoners). But for Cosgrave and his government the actions, although highly unpalatable, had the desired effect.

Yet, it was not the end of the controversial policy. In fact, over the coming days Mulcahy issued revised regulations concerning the AEPR, much to Davitt's chagrin. The JAG absolved himself and his department from the process of drafting these new regulations. Under the revised regulations, the military courts were abolished and replaced by tribunals when prisoners were found in possession of firearms or ammunition. These tribunals, made up of army officers, would adjudicate on such cases; prisoners found guilty would be sentenced to death 'or such other punishment'. The first results of these new regulations were seen on 19 December, when seven Republicans from the Rathbride column near Kildare town were shot at the detention barracks in the Curragh Camp.

The new Free State, in the view of outside representatives in Dublin, resembled a swan. Underneath the calm exterior projected by Cosgrave, O'Higgins, Mulcahy and others, the British representative argued, Republican tactics had 'succeeded in rattling the civilian supporters of the Free State'. This state of agitation and restlessness only increased as 1923 dawned. In 1924 O'Higgins told an inquiry that he was 'far from satisfied' with the performance of the National Army during the civil war, in particular their failure to protect the people who 'were entitled to [it,] from an organisation of 50,000 costing them eleven million pounds in a single year'. He was, furthermore, deeply suspicious of the clique of IRB members who remained in the army's leadership. Was this clique prolonging the conflict in a vindictive campaign to avenge their slain chief, Collins?

The number of executions, which took place in December 1922, was dwarfed by the figures for January 1923. Thirty-four executions took place across ten locations. A few of those shot had been arrested for possessing firearms. But others, especially in Kerry, were convicted of sabotaging or conspiring to sabotage local railway lines. Not all of those executed in January, moreover, had been arrested in that month. In fact, several cases had been held over since the autumn as legal argument and counter-argument had been heard. Several men, mostly in 'quiet' counties such as Donegal, were not subjected to execution despite having been found guilty of illegally possessing arms.

Five of those executed in January had deserted from the National Army at Baldonnel Aerodrome in November 1922. They subsequently joined a Republican flying column in Kildare led by Patrick Mullaney. Following engagements with National Army units in the Maynooth district in early December, in which one National Army soldier was killed, these deserters and seventeen of their colleagues were captured. The five deserters were court-martialled in Kilmainham on 11 December and executed by firing squad on 8 January 1923.

A blow to the tribunal system was dealt by the mis-handling of the investigation into the murder of O'Higgins' father Dr Thomas Higgins. Republicans killed Dr Higgins in the living room of his house near Stradbally, King's County. Shortly after his funeral a National Army sweep of Stradbally and neighbouring areas led to the arrest of several Republicans, including Martin Byrne. Byrne was tried, found guilty of Dr Higgins' murder, and sentenced to death. Yet following persistent interventions by a local Stradbally solicitor, Horace Turpin, assisted by his nephew (and future judge) T.C. Kingsmill-Moore, Byrne was retried at Portobello Barracks and found not guilty. National Army officers later admitted misidentifying Byrne in the aftermath of his arrest.

From late February, anti-Republican sentiment resurfaced within National Army ranks. Over the following month, several brutal killings were conducted in many counties, followed by a resumption of executions in the middle of March. The killings took place in counties that had seen high rates of guerrilla violence up to this point, most especially Connacht and counties Cork and Kerry.

The area bounded by the Arigna Mountains proved intensely troubling for the National Army. The London *Times* commented that the National Army in the region was 'trustworthy only in parts … a large portion of it … sympathises with the Republican cause'. Violence was therefore threefold: directed against the National Army, directed against the Republicans and directed against the pro-Republican National Army members. The major event to illustrate this was a daytime raid on Ballyconnell, Co. Cavan, on 12 February that received a hugely critical response in newspapers and on the floor of the Dáil. That morning, a force of fifty anti-Treaty IRA soldiers invaded the town. Three shops, a car dealership and the local post office were bombed and burned to the ground. Two men, William Ryan and Seán McGrath, were dragged out into the streets and shot dead. Ryan's employer, William Ovens (who owned a grocery shop) was also shot in the leg. The Ballyconnell raid was a response to the killing of Michael Cull, an anti-Treaty IRA volunteer from Roscommon, in the town on 6 January 1923.

Control of the Arigna Mountains region had been hotly contested in 1922, when near-famine conditions were reported by local authorities in Leitrim. At the time of the Ballyconnell raid, control of the region had been claimed by the anti-Treaty IRA in the guise of Ned Bofin and his brigade. Bofin had conducted raids on Carrick-on-Shannon, Dowra and Manorhamilton before staging a spectacular raid on Ballinamore barracks on 28 January 1923, when the barracks was captured and later destroyed, along with the local railway station.35 National Army members were also taken prisoner. Together with the Ballyconnell raid, the Ballinamore raid was a clear signal that Free State authority in south Leitrim and west Cavan needed to be asserted.

Speaking in the Dáil in the wake of the raids on Ballinamore and Ballyconnell, Mulcahy argued that the events disclosed 'a particular type of madness in the country', a madness that could only be dealt with by the policies the Free State government were implementing to restore law and order. Those were, in Mulcahy's words, by arresting those responsible for attacks such as Ballyconnell, 'charging them … and if they are found guilty … executing them.' A few days later Leitrim and west Cavan were declared a Special Military Area by the government, and a force of over 300 National Army soldiers under the command of Dan Hogan, equipped with motorised transport and five Lewis guns, were despatched from Dublin to the area. Over the following month both sides engaged in skirmishes across the region, before Bofin was captured on 23 March 1923. By the end of 1922, the National Army command in Cork was in many respects uncoordinated.

Emmet Dalton had departed from the command in mysterious circumstances in November 1922, and it took three months for his successor David Reynolds to be appointed. While Reynolds was generally averse to the policy of summary execution, the period of his leadership did include a few examples of retribution by National Army troops against their Republican enemies.

On 4 March 1923, a mine explosion near Newcestown killed two and injured nine others, including two National Army soldiers. The two victims, Patrick Murray and Seamus O'Leary, were described in press reports as 'Republican prisoners' who were set to work clearing barricades along a stretch of road from Newcestown to Bandon. Other statements contradicted this, claiming both men were conscripted along with other youths after mass in the village that morning.

The Newcestown killings came in a period of increased violence in Cork. A mine on the Youghal to Midleton road at Castlemartyr exploded as a convoy of National Army troops approached; although no casualties were reported, injuries were suffered. In the city the courthouse and houses in the Dillon's Cross area were bombed, again with no fatalities but injuries. Arrests and explosions dominated the headlines in the *Cork Examiner* for several weeks in February and March 1923. A major explosion on the morning of Friday 2 March severely damaged St Mary's Hall, located across the road from the cathedral of SS Mary & Anne on Cork city's northside. Four people were injured, two severely. Three men were detained close to the scene. One motive for the explosion was the failure of hall management to close in solidarity with other entertainment venues (St Mary's was a noted picture house in the locality) during the hunger strike of Anne MacSwiney in Kilmainham Gaol.

In Kerry, revenge killings were a hallmark of the war from September 1922 onwards. Late in the month a National Army officer was killed in a skirmish on the bridge at Castlemaine. A few days later, a Republican attack on Killorglin was rebuffed, despite Republicans outnumbering their National Army counterparts by about eight to one. In follow-up operations by the National Army, prisoners were taken and one prisoner, John Galvin, admitted to the Castlemaine killing while in custody. Galvin was shot in the head and his body dumped in Ballyseedy Wood to the south-east of Tralee. But this was not the most controversial incident to happen in these woods.

Despite O'Daly's previous assertions regarding the treatment of political prisoners, some of the most controversial incidents of the entire war happened in the space of about a week in the early spring of 1923. On Thursday 22 February, a detachment of Dublin Guards (attached to the National Army and stationed in Ballymullen Barracks in Tralee) was fired upon at Castlemaine while proceeding to Killorglin. Two soldiers were injured, and the attackers escaped under the cover of darkness. Just over a week later, on Monday 5 March, a large battle was fought between Republicans and National Army troops near Cahirciveen. Two Republicans and three National Army soldiers were

Paddy O'Daly, Eoin O'Duffy and Richard Mulcahy inspecting the Dublin Guard unit of the Free State Army at Beggars Bush Barracks.

killed, and both sides suffered injuries. The National Army also captured seven prisoners.

On the morning after the Cahirciveen battle, a squad of Dublin Guards travelled from Tralee to Knocknagoshel. Their mission was to recover a cache of arms and ammunition dumped by Republicans near Barrinang Wood. While removing the arms, a trap mine, which was part of the dump, exploded. Captains Michael Dunne and Joseph Stapleton, along with Lieut P. O'Connor and two privates were killed. It was later claimed by Republicans that O'Connor had been the chief target of this booby trap, given his central role in torturing Republican prisoners in the county. Whether O'Daly formally issued orders in the wake of the Knocknagoshel killings to use Republican prisoners as human minesweepers is contested, but there is no doubt that this policy quickly bore controversial fruit.

The following night, another detachment of Dublin Guards was travelling from Tralee to Killorglin when they encountered extensive barricades in the vicinity of Ballyseedy Wood three miles southeast of the town. Returning to town, they commandeered nine prisoners held at Ballymullen Barracks. What transpired once the party of troops and prisoners returned to Ballyseedy remains one of the most controversial incidents of the entire war. According to contemporary newspaper reports, the prisoners were working to clear the barricades when a trap mine exploded, killing eight of the nine.

Unsurprisingly, these reports were heavily challenged and disputed by Republicans at the time and subsequently. The most harrowing and vivid published account of Ballyseedy came from Dorothy Macardle in her *Tragedies of Kerry*:

> The lorry pulled up near the corner of the Killorglin Road, beside Ballyseedy Wood. They saw a log lying across the road. They were made to get out of the lorry and stand in a close circle around the log.
>
> The soldiers had strong ropes and electric cord. Each prisoner's hands were tied behind him, then his arms were tied above the elbow to those of the men on either side of him. Their feet were bound together above the ankles and their legs were bound together above the knees. Then a strong rope was passed round the mine and the soldiers moved away.
>
> The prisoners had their backs to the log and the mine, which was beside it; they could see the movement of the soldiers and knew what would happen next. They gripped one another's hands, those who could, and prayed for God's mercy upon their souls.

The shock came, blinding, deafening, overwhelming. For Stephen Fuller [the sole surviving prisoner] it was followed by a silence in which he knew he was alive. Then sounds came to him – cries and low moans, then the sounds of rifle fire and exploding bombs. Then silence again: the work was done.

The bodies of the prisoners were returned to Ballymullen and released to their families on the following day. It was, in the words of the *Cork Examiner* correspondent present, 'a painful process'.

Although listed amongst those who had been killed in the explosion at Ballyseedy, Stephen Fuller of Kilflynn, Lixnaw, survived the explosion, albeit sustaining severe

Members of the IRA in Kerry 1922 – Stephen Fuller is standing in the back row, second from the left. Others include standing Dennis Connell, Willie Hartnett, Timmie Tuomey (killed at Ballyseedy); front row – Terry Brosnan, John McElligot, D. O'Shea, Timothy Aero Lyons, Pete Sullivan and Paddy Mahony.

injuries from being thrown several hundred yards away by the force of the blast. He was treated by Dr Shanahan from Farranfore. Fuller later recalled in a TV interview before his death that the skin covering his hands and the back of his legs was badly burned as a result of the explosion. In the same testimony Fuller also remembered a National Army soldier telling him and his colleagues to say hello to some dead comrades of his if they ended up in heaven. More seriously, he also told of National Army soldiers opening fire on the wounded men following the explosion, to make sure they were dead. In later life Ned Breslin, the officer in charge of the National Army troops at Ballyseedy, married the sister of George O'Shea, one of the victims. On one of his frequent visits to Kerry he entered a pub one night that Fuller happened to be in. Fuller finished his drink, got up and left.

Ballyseedy was replicated, albeit to a smaller degree, at Countess Bridge near Killarney the following day. A trap mine killed four Republican prisoners on that occasion. A few days later, a third mine explosion at Cahirciveen killed five Republicans. All three incidents bore the hallmarks of reprisal attacks by Dublin Guards soldiers, especially for the killings at Knocknagoshel. Mulcahy ordered an inquiry into the killings, which was carried out by O'Daly in quick order.

When the report was published, the National Army soldiers were exonerated, much to the fury of the families of the victims and prominent Republicans in the county such as John Joe Sheehy. Some National Army officers in the county were also annoyed at the attempted cover-up. Niall Harrington, who had been stationed in the county since the Fenit landings the previous August, carried out his own unofficial inquiries, but his findings went unpublished. Lieut McCarthy, a National Army officer serving in the county, later resigned from the army, stating that the Cahirciveen incidents were wilful murder: 'the prisoners were shot first and then put over a mine and blown up'.

Events at Knocknagoshel, Ballyseedy, Castlemaine, Countess Bridge and Cahirciveen were the subject of much recrimination on both sides in the aftermath of the atrocities, and still to this day provoke emotional responses. Five Republican prisoners captured during the abortive attack on Cahirciveen on 5 March were executed at the end of that month, doing little to reduce the ill-feeling.

In April, a prominent IRA commander in north Kerry, Timothy 'Aeroplane' Lyons, was killed when his hiding place near Kerry Head (north-west of Ballyheigue and Banna Strand) was surrounded by National Army forces. Later that month a large sweep in the south of the county led to the major Republican forces in the county being confined to the high ground east of the Kenmare-Kilgarvan-Killarney road. The final event in Kerry before the Aiken's order was more executions: four survivors of the siege at Kerry Head, along with men from Ballyduff, were killed at Ballymullen Barracks on 25 April.

The controversies in Kerry, and to a lesser extent Cork and Connacht, added to the struggles experienced by National Army officers in counties such as Wexford, demonstrated that the decision in January 1923 to increase the scope of the AEPR to include death sentences for offences ranging from openly assisting anti-Treaty IRA forces to deserting from the National Army was justified. In the six weeks from the middle of March to the end of April 1923, Republican prisoners in Wexford, Dublin, Cork, Westmeath, and Donegal were executed. Recent research into these executions has argued that power struggle between the Executive Council and the Army Council was responsible to a large degree for the increase. The Executive Council saw that the National Army was fast-becoming ungovernable and unaccountable. Yet, this policy did not stem the tide of unsanctioned killings. By the end of March, twelve Republicans in the custody of the National Army had been killed.

An increase in executions was met by Republicans in some areas with reprisals, not against the National Army *per se*, but against alleged informers. This paranoia, which gripped parts of the country towards the ending of the Truce, resurfaced with haunting resonances. One example of this was the killing of sixteen-year-old Ben McCarthy from Bantry in the early hours of Monday 19 March. At approximately 4 a.m., McCarthy was taken from his home; four hours later, his body was discovered by a National Army patrol on a road near Lough Bofinna, three miles east of the town. A coroners' inquest later that day in the town heard evidence that his body had several bullet wounds in it, and a sign was placed on the corpse reading: 'Convicted spy. Shot as a reprisal for the execution of our comrades during the week.' A verdict of wilful murder was returned.

Despite this painful remembrance of dark times, Free State attention turned from the conduct of military operations against Republicans to other matters of pressing concern. For example, the destruction of transport networks, especially railway lines, had a huge effect on the conduct of business and commerce in certain regions. In the initial months of the war areas of Tipperary, Limerick and Louth were effectively cut off due to the railways in those areas being damaged. Kerry and most of Connacht were without functioning rail lines for much of war. To remedy this a Railroad Protection and Maintenance Corps (RPMC) was established in October 1922. Despite documented struggles to obtain supplies, the RPMC conducted its task admirably, and by the end of May 1923 all bar three lines (the Rosslare-Waterford-Mallow line and two small branch lines from Skibbereen to Schull and Skibbereen to Baltimore) were operating.

A final controversial aspect of the Civil War concerned the treatment of Republican prisoners. Over the period from June 1921 to June 1923 National Army or Civic Guard forces captured some 5,000 Republicans. The most pressing concern of authorities at the beginning of the war was where to detain prisoners. A variety of formal prisons, barracks and makeshift internment camps were used to house them.

Mountjoy Jail was the main military prison used by the Provisional Government to detain the highest-level

Republican prisoners. Shortly after the fall of the Four Courts, riots broke out in the prison. Diarmuid O'Hegarty, the prison governor, gave permission for his troops to shoot any prisoners attempting to escape or resist arrest. Controversially, he also ordered troops to disperse protestors gathered outside the jail by force. On 6 July 1922, troops fired into a crowd gathered outside, killing one person.

The Provisional Government debated this incident a few days later. The decision to release as many 'rank and file' Republican prisoners was swiftly taken to create more space. Further space was created by the reopening of Kilmainham Gaol with Seán Ó Muirthuile as governor. The use of Gormanstown Camp in Co. Meath was offered by the British army and reluctantly accepted. Further plans were very briefly discussed to transport prisoners to the Seychelles and Saint Helena. The opening of the Curragh Camp later in the year with its projected 12,000 prison spaces partially eased the pressure.

A good example of the problems the government and National Army faced in dealing with Republican prisoners came in Athlone. The lack of firm control by the army over Galway city at the start of war meant that all Republicans detained in Connacht were to be transferred to Custume Barracks, as well as those detained in western Leinster.

The actual prison quarters in the barracks were soon full; further detainees had to be incarcerated in what amount to little more than guarded camps. The *Irish Independent* detailed conditions: 'inmates … had to sleep on makeshift beds and be content with a very restricted diet', all the while being abused by recent National Army recruits 'who were never in the Volunteers, and [were] always hostile to the Republic'. Patrick Morrissey further alleged that men were refused medical treatment and visitation rights.

On 6 October 1922 Capt. Patrick Mulrennan of Ballaghaderreen, an IRA prisoner at Custume, was shot and killed by Brig.-Gen. Lawlor. The killing sparked outrage on both sides.

Locking up reluctant prisoners in sub-standard prison accommodation only proved a recipe for jailbreaks and attacks on the prison. In mid-August 1922 Republican prisoners gained possession of an explosive device which they ignited and placed near a boundary wall. The ensuing explosion was heard throughout the town, and rumours quickly spread that a major attack had been launched on the barracks. However, despite this no prisoners escaped.

Over the winter of 1922–3 the number of inmates at Custume had swelled to 950. Republican publications continued to detail the conditions endured by the inmates there. Female Republican prisoners were detained separately at nearby Adamson Castle. Nevertheless, attempts at escape increased: tunnels, knotted blankets and missing table legs all testified to the variety of ways employed by prisoners in search of freedom. A hunger strike involving over 600 prisoners lasted several weeks. Again, various Republican newspapers detailed the treatment meted out by National Army officers including MacEoin, who was alleged to have taken pot-shots at prisoners with his pistol!

Women prisoners were as equally poorly treated, if not more so. In the autumn of 1922 Maud Gonne and Charlotte Despard founded the Women's Prisoners Defence League (WPDL) to protest the treatment of Republican prisoners. They held weekly protest rallies amongst the ruins of O'Connell Street and were, in the words of one historian, a 'decided embarrassment' to Cosgrave's government. At one such rally in November 1922, called to protest the detention of Mary MacSwiney (who had been arrested on the same day as Ernie O'Malley), a contingent of National Army troops fired into the crowd. Fourteen people were injured by gunshots, and at least one hundred others sustained minor injuries in the ensuing stampede.

In January 1923 many of the leading figures in the WPDL – including Gonne, Dorothy Macardle, Grace Gifford Plunkett, Mary MacSwiney and Kate O'Callaghan – were arrested and detained in Kilmainham Jail. They and prisoners in other jails regularly and strenuously protested their detention and the conditions; at one stage bedding was thrown from the windows of many cells in Kilmainham. Máire Comerford recalled a prison guard shooting her in the leg. Frequent hunger strikes took place, the longest lasting a week and involving 91 prisoners.

The climax to this period of protest came in April 1923, when plans to transfer 238 female prisoners from Mountjoy and Kilmainham to the North Dublin Union were strongly and violently resisted. Many women were dragged from their cells and down metal stairs or thrown down the stairs. Reports of sexual abuse, stripping prisoners naked and beating them were also made. Some of the violence inflicted came at the hands of members of Cumann na Saoirse; other prisoners later alleged that the 'Oriel House gang' were involved in beating up women. Following extensive publicity generated by the riots, several prisoners were released, including Mary MacSwiney and Kate O'Callaghan, who had been on hunger strike at the time of the riots.

Even after May 1923, the treatment of prisoners by the Free State did not improve. Prisoners were poorly treated, while pressure to disown their loyalty to the Republic was increased. After months of internal debate Republican prisoners in Mountjoy began a hunger strike on 13 October. In short time some 8,000 prisoners across the state were refusing to take food. Aiken, though sceptical of the effectiveness of the strike, supported it fully, telling prisoners in Kilmainham: 'I believe your fight will do more for the cause than a thousand years war'.

Despite this outward optimism unease among Republicans about the strike remained, particularly about how it was received outside the walls of the various jails. The deaths of two Cork Republican prisoners, Dinny Barry and Andy O'Sullivan, hastened the end of the strike. On 23 November 1923, following news that several Mountjoy prisoners had broken the strike, it was called off. In the weeks following, several prisoners were released, but O'Higgins objected to a full-scale release. Within six months, however, most prisoners had been released.

As much as the executions (which by the end of the war numbered eighty-three) poisoned relations between 'Free Staters' and Republicans, the treatment of prisoners further soured feelings both inside and outside the Republican tent. Taken together, both contributed significantly to the decades of bitterness and omerta which followed.

The Civil War remains a decisive and divisive period in modern Irish history. Its effects are still with us today. But it is to be hoped that the coming centenary will bring fresh impetus to understand why it happened.

Biographies

Frank Aiken (1898–1983) was born in Co. Armagh and began managing the family farm at 13. Becoming a member of Sinn Féin and the Irish Volunteers while still a teenager, he was elected local company captain, as well as serving in several local and national positions within Sinn Féin. Appointed commandant of the IRA Fourth Northern Division from March 1921, he remained in the army following the truce and worked hard to avoid the civil war. Subsequently opposed the Treaty and served in IRA GHQ, succeeding Lynch as chief-of-staff on 20 April 1923. After the war, Aiken followed De Valera out of Sinn Féin and was a founder of Fianna Fáil. He served in various governments from 1932, most prominently as Minister for Foreign Affairs.

Richard ('Dick') Barrett (1889–1922) was born near Ballineen, Co. Cork, and trained as national schoolteacher. He was prominent in GAA and Gaelic League circles in west Cork, and joined the Irish Volunteers in 1917, becoming IRA quartermaster of the Cork No. 3 Brigade. By the time of the truce, he was serving in IRA GHQ. Opposing the Treaty, he became assistant quartermaster to Liam Mellows and served in the Four Courts. After the fall of the courts, he was imprisoned in Mountjoy where, on the morning of 8 December, he was executed by firing squad. His body was returned to west Cork in November 1924, when he was reinterred in Ahiohill churchyard.

Tom Barry (1897–1980) was born in Killorglin, Co. Kerry, and subsequently grew up in Rosscarbery, Co. Cork. Having served in Mesopotamia in the British Army during the First World War, he returned to west Cork and joined the IRA, becoming a celebrated leader of the flying column of the Cork No. 3 Brigade. Barry vehemently opposed the Treaty and played a leading role in the IRA post-Truce and post-Civil War.

Robert Barton (1881–1975) was born in Co. Wicklow and educated in England. Serving in the British Army at the outbreak of the First World War, he resigned in 1916 and returned to Ireland, subsequently joining the IRA, and serving as a minister in the first Dáil governments from 1919. He was appointed by De Valera as one of the plenipotentiaries to negotiate a settlement with Lloyd George's government and signed the Treaty along with his colleagues. He subsequently opposed the Treaty and served briefly in the Hammam Hotel. After his release from prison in December 1923, he remained a supporter of De Valera and later Fianna Fáil.

Louisa ('Louie') Bennett (1870–1956) was born in Rathgar, Dublin, and educated in Blackrock and London. In 1911 she founded the Irishwomen's Suffrage Federation and was also a founding member of the Irish Women's Reform League. Assisted in the relief effort during the 1913 Lockout. After 1916 she reorganised the

Irish Women Workers' Union. It was in this capacity she acted as a mediator during the Civil War. Later she served on the executive of the Irish Trades Union Congress (ITUC) for eleven years, becoming president in 1932.

Erskine Childers (1870–1922) was born in London but grew up in Co. Wicklow, a cousin of Robert Barton. Educated in London he fought in the First World War but joined the fledgling Sinn Féin shortly after the war. He served as publicity director for the Volunteers, and after the truce was a plenipotentiary in London though, like his cousin, he subsequently rejected the settlement. His talents as a propagandist saw him targeted by the pro-Treaty administration. On 10 November 1922, he was arrested in Barton's home after a skirmish with an arresting party. Two weeks later, he was executed by firing squad.

Kathleen (Daly) Clarke (1878–1972) was born in Limerick into a prominent Fenian family. Apprenticed to a seamstress, she later started her own dressmaking business. Through her uncle John Daly, she was introduced to Tom Clarke in 1898. Three years later she emigrated to New York, where she married Clarke and later ran a shop and a market garden on Long Island. In 1907 the couple returned to Dublin, opening a tobacconist shop in first Amiens Street and later Parnell Street. Kathleen immersed herself in the Irish Republican Brotherhood (IRB) and assisted with the production of the Brotherhood's newspaper *Irish Freedom*. In 1914 she attended the inaugural meeting of Cumann na mBan, later becoming the president of the central branch. In 1916 she was imprisoned briefly in Dublin Castle and suffered the loss of her husband and brother Edward, who were both executed. Later, she served on the Sinn Féin executive and was a vice-president of Cumann na mBan. She was elected to the Dáil in 1921. Voted against the Treaty but chaired the Dáil committee attempting to prevent the split, which was unsuccessful. After the war she left Sinn Féin to join Fianna Fáil, serving as TD (1927) and Senator (1928–36). In 1941 she left Fianna Fáil and ran as a Clann na Poblachta candidate in the 1948 general election. She emigrated to Liverpool in 1965 where she died in 1972. After a state funeral in the pro-cathedral in Dublin, she was buried in Deansgrange Cemetery.

Michael Collins (1890–1922) was born near Lisavaird, Co. Cork and educated in Clonakilty. By the start of the War of Independence he was a minister in the Dáil cabinet and Director of Intelligence and Organisation for the IRA. He was also recognised as president of the Irish Republic by the IRB. A co-leader of the delegation in London with Arthur Griffith, he reluctantly signed the Treaty on 6 December 1922. Appointed head of the Provisional Government in January 1922, and Minister for Defence and *de jure* commander-in-chief of the National Army. Killed in an ambush at Beál na Bláth, Co. Cork, on 22 August 1922 and buried in Glasnevin Cemetery.

Mary Eva (Máire) Comerford (1893–1982) was born in Rathdrum, Co. Wicklow, where her family ran a mill and were friends with the Parnells. Educated privately, she was sent to England after her father's death to train as a secretary. While there she became interested in Irish history and politics. She returned to Ireland to assist her mother run a school at Courtown, Co. Wexford. While visiting relatives in Dublin in Easter 1916, she witnessed first-hand the Rising and was radicalised. She joined Sinn Féin in Wexford in 1916 and Cumann na mBan in 1917. The following year she moved to Dublin to work as a secretary for the historian Alice Stopford Green, although this relationship did not last very long due to increasing political differences. Comerford campaigned for Sinn Féin in December 1918 and during the War of Independence worked as a Cumann na mBan organiser and a dispatch carrier for the IRA in Louth, Armagh and Down. She opposed the Treaty and served in the Four Courts. In 1923 she was arrested after an abortive attempt to kidnap W.T. Cosgrave and imprisoned in Mountjoy. She escaped on 9 May 1923, was rearrested on 1 June and released to a nursing home three weeks later after a prolonged hunger strike. After campaigning for Sinn Féin in Cork during the general election, she was sent to the USA on a fundraising mission. Returning to Ireland the following year, she settled on a poultry farm in Wexford. In 1926 she was elected to the Sinn Féin executive. A little over a decade later she was made editor of the 'Woman's Page' of the *Irish Press*, a position she held until her retirement in 1964. She died in 1982 at Sandyford and buried near Gorey.

William Thomas ('W.T.') Cosgrave (1880–1965) was born in Dublin and left school at 16 to work in the family public house. In 1905, he joined the fledgling Sinn Féin party, and three years later was elected to Dublin Corporation. During the Easter Rising, he was part of the occupying force in the South Dublin Union. Shortly after his release from prison in 1917, he was elected MP for Kilkenny City, and for North Kilkenny at the general election the following year. He served as Minister for Local Government in the Dáil cabinet, and in the Treaty debate supported the pro-Treaty side. After the deaths of Griffith and Collins Cosgrave became chairman of the Provisional Government. On 6 December 1922, he became president of the Executive Council of the Irish Free State, holding this position until 1932. He was a founding member of Cumann na nGaedheal, and in 1933 became chairman of the new Fine Gael party, a post he occupied until his retirement from politics in 1944.

(James) Emmet Dalton (1898–1978) was born in Fall River, Massachusetts, before emigrating with his family to Dublin in 1900. Having joined the Irish Volunteers in 1913, Dalton joined the British Army in 1916, serving alongside Irish Party MP Tom Kettle in France and seeing action in Palestine. After his demobilisation in 1919 he returned to Dublin, joining the IRB and IRA shortly after. He acted as a liaison officer for Michael Collins and led a daring if unsuccessful attempt to spring Seán MacEoin from Mountjoy Jail. After the truce, he was part of the delegation to London, arranging for a special plane to fly Collins home in the event of a breakdown in the negotiations. Having accepted the Treaty, he became Director of Military Operations for the National Army. He masterminded the seaborne landings in Cork and Kerry in August 1922 and accompanied Collins on his final fatal tour of Co. Cork. Collins' death and the circumstances surrounding it affected Dalton deeply and, combined with psychological after-effects he suffered following the First World War, he began to drink heavily. Therefore, his performance in command of the National Army suffered. He resigned his commission in the army on 9 December 1922, taking up a new role as clerk of the Seanad for three years. In later years, Dalton became a film producer, being one of the founders of Ardmore Studios in Bray, Co. Wicklow.

Cahir Davitt (1894–1986) was born in Dublin, son of the famous political figure Michael Davitt. He was educated at several schools in Dublin and attended UCD from 1911 to 1916, graduating first with a BA and then a law degree. He was called to the bar in January 1916 and later practised on the Munster and Connacht circuits. He joined the Irish Volunteers in 1915 and during the War of Independence was one of two circuit judges of the Dáil Courts. Having served as judge advocate general in the National Army, Davitt was appointed first as an assistant and then as a full circuit court judge for Dublin, serving until 1945. In 1945, he was appointed as a high court judge, serving as its president from 1951 to 1966. He also served as president of the Leinster branch of the IRFU, and later of the IRFU itself, as well as being a long-serving member of its executive.

Éamon de Valera (1882–1975) at the time of the truce was president of Dáil Éireann, having served in the Irish Volunteers and as commandant of the Boland's Mills garrison during the Easter Rising. After the signing of the Treaty, he became leader of the anti-Treaty faction of Sinn Féin. In 1925, he resigned from Sinn Féin, founding Fianna Fáil in 1926. The following year he led the party into the Free State Dáil, and five years later won a general election, becoming president of the Executive Council. In 1938, the electorate approved a new constitution, which he heavily wrote. Having served as Taoiseach from 1938 to 1948 and again from 1951 to 1954 and from 1957 to 1959, he was elected as president of Ireland, a post he held until 1973.

Liam Deasy (1896–1974) was born in Kilmacsimon Quay, Co. Cork, and was educated locally until he left school at thirteen. Active in the Gaelic League and the GAA in his youth, he joined the Irish Volunteers in 1916, being sworn into the IRB the following year. In August 1919, he was promoted to adjutant of the IRA Cork

No. 3 Brigade and spent the War of Independence as an organiser while 'on the run'. In March 1921, he was elected commanding officer of the brigade. A year later, he assumed command of the IRA First Southern Division. He reluctantly took the anti-Treaty side and worked closely with Liam Lynch. After his arrest in January 1923, he controversially appealed to his comrades to surrender. The following year he was expelled from the IRA. In later life, he was a successful businessman, briefly serving as a commandant in the Irish Defence Forces during The Emergency. He was working on a sequel to his successful book *Towards Ireland Free* (published in 1973), entitled *Brother against Brother*, by the time of his death.

Eamonn Duggan (1874–1936) was born in Co. Meath and qualified as a solicitor. Having served in the North Dublin Union during the Easter Rising, Duggan was imprisoned but able to resume his legal practice after his release the following year. A senior member of the IRB, Duggan served as IRA Director of Intelligence for two and a half years. He was arrested in November 1920 and imprisoned in Mountjoy; it was here in the company of Arthur Griffith that the process leading to the truce and Treaty began. On his release, he served as liaison officer for De Valera, accompanying him to London in his negotiations with Lloyd George. He was part of the Treaty delegation and supported it during the Treaty Debates in the Dáil (he was TD for Louth-Meath at the time). Duggan served in the

Provisional Government and later as parliamentary secretary to several ministers in the Executive Council from 1922 to 1932. In the years before his sudden death, he served as a Free State Senator and as chairman of Dún Laoghaire borough council.

George Gavan Duffy (1882–1951) was born in Rock Ferry, Cheshire, and was educated in England and France before qualifying as a solicitor in 1907. Through his wife Margaret, the daughter of A.M. Sullivan, he met many members of the early Sinn Féin. It was his work as defence counsel for Sir Roger Casement in 1916 that radicalised him to the cause of Irish nationalism. He moved to Dublin shortly after the trial ended, being called to the Irish Bar in 1917 and being elected Sinn Féin MP for Dublin County South the following year. He served as an envoy of Dáil Éireann in Paris and then Rome, before his appointment as a plenipotentiary to London by De Valera in October 1921. He supported the Treaty and was made Minister for External Affairs in the Provisional Government, only to resign in protest in July 1922 after the abolition of the Dáil Courts. Thereafter he opposed the Treaty settlement. Originally De Valera's first choice for attorney general in 1932, his original support for the Treaty counted against him. He later served as a high court judge, and from 1946 until his death was its president.

Edith (Maud) Gonne (MacBride) (1866–1953) was born in Surrey and lived most of her life between England, Ireland and France. By 1886 she was a committed

Irish nationalist, moving in the same circles as George Russell, Stephen Gwynn, Douglas Hyde and WB Yeats. In the 1890s she became closely involved with Arthur Griffith and took an active part in many of his campaigns. In 1903 she married Boer War veteran Major John MacBride; their son, Seán, was born in Paris the following year. Although they divorced shortly afterwards, MacBride's execution reawakened Gonne's radicalism. She was arrested in 1918 but released shortly after. During the War of Independence, she was involved with the Irish White Cross. Although she initially accepted the Treaty and worked to avoid a military war, following Griffith's death she rejected it and was imprisoned twice in 1923. After the war she involved herself in prisoners' rights movements in Ireland and abroad. She died in 1953 and was buried in Glasnevin cemetery.

Arthur Griffith (1871–1922) was born in Dublin and worked as a journalist until after his arrest in the aftermath of the Easter Rising. Elected as MP for East Cavan in early 1918 while in jail as part of the 'German Plot' arrests, he was vice-president of Dáil Éireann until his arrest in November 1920. While in Mountjoy Jail he, Eamonn Duggan and others, engaged in clandestine talks with Dublin Castle officials, including Alfred Cope, which paved the way for the Truce in July 1921. De Valera appointed Griffith to lead the delegation to London in October 1921, and he was the first to sign the Treaty on 6 December 1921. Thereafter he became one of the staunchest supporters of the settlement. He was elected Dáil Éireann president in succession to De Valera and fought hard to reconcile the factions of Sinn Féin. He died suddenly of a brain haemorrhage in Dublin on 12 August 1922 and was buried in Glasnevin.

Niall Charles Harrington (1901–1981) was born in Dublin, son of then Lord Mayor Timothy Charles Harrington. After his father's death, he was raised in Tralee, and educated at the local CBS and in Rockwell College, Co. Tipperary. In 1918, he started an apprenticeship in pharmaceutical chemist in Boyle, Co. Roscommon. While in the town he joined the Irish Volunteers and later the IRA. Forced to leave the town two years later, he returned to Dublin and joined the IRA there. In March 1922, he joined the new National Army, becoming a corporal shortly afterwards. He served at the Four Courts and on Sackville Street in the early weeks of the Civil War. In August, he accompanied the Dublin Guards at their landing at Fenit, Co. Kerry. He joined the Guards shortly after, serving in Kerry for the remainder of the war. He later served in army GHQ, the Military Archives, and as deputy director of Army Intelligence. His memoir of his Civil War experiences in Kerry, *Kerry Landing*, was published posthumously in 1992.

Sighle/Sheila (Mary Ellen) Humphreys (Bean Uí Dhonnachadha) (1899–1994) was born in Limerick, niece of Michael Joseph ('The') O'Rahilly. In her youth she was heavily influenced by her outspoken nationalist aunt Áine. The family moved to Dublin in 1909 where she was educated in Mount Anville and Lower Leeson Street. Having participated in pre-Rising activities of the Irish Volunteers, Humphreys joined Cumann na mBan in 1919 and during the War of Independence carried out messenger duties and organisational work in Kerry in 1921. She developed a friendship with Liam Mellows, whose socialist views she shared. Having taken the anti-Treaty side, she was head of the cortege at the funeral of Cathal Brugha. In November 1922 Humphreys was arrested along with Ernie O'Malley and the Rahilly family. She was imprisoned in Mountjoy, Kilmainham and the North Dublin Union. Released in 1923, she resumed her work with Cumann na mBan, becoming director of publicity in 1926. In 1935 she married Donal O'Donoghue; the couple had one daughter. In the 1930s she was active in Saor Eire; in the 1940s with Clann na Poblachta; in the 1960s she opposed Irish entry of the EEC; in the 1970s she sat on the Dublin Housing Committee; and in the 1980s she supported Sinn Féin and the H-Block hunger strikers. Along with this, she devoted much of her adult life to work with St Vincent de Paul in Dublin's Inner City. She died in March 1994.

Rosamund Jacob (1888–1960) was born in Waterford into a Quaker family with strong nationalist and republican links. In her youth she was involved with the Irish National League, the Gaelic League and

Inighinidhe na hÉireann (Daughters of Erin), before becoming a founder member of Sinn Féin in the city in 1906. Later she also joined the Irish Women's Franchise League and Cumann na mBan. In 1917 she served as a delegate from Waterford to the Sinn Féin convention. In 1920 she moved to Dublin, lodging with Hannah Sheehy-Skeffington. During the Civil War she opposed the Treaty but worked with Maud Gonne's peace movement and the WPDL; she was briefly imprisoned in 1923. In 1926 she resigned from Sinn Féin and joined Fianna Fáil. She spent the remainder of her life writing and publishing, producing fiction and historical works. In October 1960 she died in Dublin's Meath Hospital having been knocked down in a road accident.

Liam Lynch (1893–1923) was born in Co. Limerick and apprenticed to a hardware business at Mitchelstown. In 1917, he organised a company of the Irish Volunteers in Fermoy and was elected adjutant of the battalion. He became commandant of the Cork No. 2 Brigade of the IRA in January 1919, leading the brigade in a series of actions during the War of Independence. In April 1921, the First Southern Division was formed, with Lynch as its commandant. A long-time member of the IRB, he was the only member of its Supreme Council to vote against the Treaty. In March 1922, he was elected IRA chief-of-staff following a convention composed mostly of anti-Treaty supporters. During the Civil War, he favoured a strategy of containment rather than confrontation, and even in the later months of the war maintained a strident stance in favour of continuing the fighting. On 10 April 1923, he was shot in a skirmish with National Army forces on the slopes of the Knockmealdown Mountains in Co. Tipperary, dying in Clonmel later that evening. He was buried in Kilcrumper Cemetery near Fermoy.

Dorothy Macardle (1889–1958) was born in Dundalk, Co. Louth, and was educated at home and later in Dublin. Having graduated from the National University of Ireland in 1912, she qualified as a teacher in 1914. After two years in Stratford-upon-Avon, Macardle returned to Dublin in 1917 where she worked in Alexandra College and was prominent in local theatre circles. There she befriended Maude Gonne and Constance Markievicz, and came to know De Valera. She joined Cumann na mBan in either 1918 or 1919, and worked with Erskine Childers, Gonne, and Charlotte Despard in propagandising Sinn Féin and supporting prisoners' dependents and widows. She was sacked from her teaching job in 1922 for her political activities and was arrested later that year. While in Mountjoy Jail she took part in a hunger strike, which severely weakened her health. Her commitment to the Republican cause continued unwavering after her release in May 1923. The following year she published *Tragedies of Kerry*, based on eyewitness accounts of the atrocities committed by the Dublin Guards in the county during the Civil War. In 1926, she was a founder member of Fianna Fáil, and later worked as the drama critic for the *Irish Press*. During this time, she set about collecting documents and reminiscences of the War of Independence and Civil War period. The finished book, *The Irish Republic*, was published in 1937. She later lived in England during the Second World War but returned to Dublin and continued her career as a writer and journalist. She died in Drogheda in 1958.

Seán MacEoin (1893–1973) was born near Granard, Co. Longford, and educated locally. Apprenticed to his father, a blacksmith, he took over the business in 1913. The following year he joined the local corps of the Irish Volunteers and was sworn into the IRB. Five years later, he was appointed O/C of the First Battalion of the Longford IRA Brigade. The following year he was promoted to vice-O/C of the brigade and became provincial centre for the IRB, with a seat on the brotherhood's Supreme Council. During the War of Independence, he conducted several operations in Longford. Arrested in March 1921, he was released the following August. Elected TD for Longford-Westmeath in May 1921, MacEoin supported the Treaty in the debates, joining the newly formed National Army shortly after. In June 1922, he was appointed overall commander of the army's Western Command based in Athlone. After the war, he remained in the army, serving as commander in the Curragh Camp, quartermaster general and chief-of-staff. He resigned in 1929 to contest a by-election in Leitrim-Sligo, where he was elected. He was a Cumann na nGaedheal/Fine Gael TD for Longford from 1932 to 1965, serving as Minister for Justice from 1948 to 1951 and Minister for Defence from 1954 to 1957. He also stood unsuccessfully in two presidential elections, 1945 and 1959.

Mary MacSwiney (1872–1942) was born in London, moving to Cork city with her family at the age of seven. Suffering from ill health in her childhood (which culminated in her foot being amputated), she did not complete formal schooling until the age of twenty. By the age of twenty-eight she was teaching in a few English convent schools before returning to Cork in 1904, where she taught at St Angela's Ursuline convent. She graduated from UCC with a BA in 1912. In 1911, she was a founder member of the Munster Women's Franchise League, and three years later she founded a branch of Cumann na mBan in the city. She was arrested in her classroom in the aftermath of the Easter Rising but released shortly after. She was elected to Cumann na mBan's national executive in 1917 and worked to support her brother Terence in his activities. His death in October 1920 propelled her into national prominence. In May 1921, she was elected TD for Cork City and during the Treaty debates showed her uncompromising support for the Republican cause. During the Civil War, she worked as a non-combatant supporting the IRA. After the war, she played a leading role in the bitter debate which culminated in De Valera leaving Sinn Féin in 1925. In her later life, she joined the IRA and continued to work for the Republican ideal.

Constance Georgine (Gore-Booth) Markievicz (1868–1927) was born in London but grew up in the family home, Lisadell House in Co. Sligo. She was educated at home, but later toured Europe with her sister and was presented to Queen Victoria at Buckingham Palace in 1887. Studying art at the Slade School in London, she moved to Paris in 1898 to further these studies. While there she met Casmir Dunin-Markievicz, son of a Polish count. In 1900 the couple were married in London, and a daughter, Maeve, was born the following year; she was sent to Sligo to be raised by her grandparents. The couple divorced in 1909, shortly after Constance had moved to Dublin. There, she joined Sinn Féin and Inighinidhe na hÉireann (INH). By 1911 she was a member of the executives of both organisations, and two years later she was honorary treasurer of the Irish Citizen Army (ICA). The following year she helped merge some branches of INH into the new Cumann na mBan. She opposed Irish involvement in the First World War, and during the Rising commanded a detachment of ICA in St Stephen's Green. Imprisoned afterwards (a death sentence was commuted on account of her gender) she was released in 1917, returning to Dublin and converting to Catholicism. Later that year she was elected to the Sinn Féin executive. Arrested the following year, she was elected to the First Dáil and appointed Minister for Labour. In 1922 she denounced the Treaty and used her presidency of Cumann na mBan (and the children's movement, Fianna Éireann) to organise opposition. She was arrested and imprisoned in 1923 but released shortly after. In 1926 she broke with Sinn Féin and Cumann na mBan and joined Fianna Fáil. Her health declined quickly in 1927 and she died shortly after being elected a Fianna Fáil TD. She was buried in Glasnevin.

Joe McKelvey (1898–1922) was born in Stewartstown, Co. Tyrone, and educated locally. He qualified as an accountant and worked for a time in Belfast. In 1919, he joined the IRB and the IRA in Belfast, as well as being prominent in GAA and Gaelic League circles. During the War of Independence, he commanded the Belfast Brigade, organising the killing of Detective Oswald Swanzy in Lisburn. Despite the truce in July 1921 fighting continued between the IRA and the new Northern Irish police force, the B Specials. After the signing of the Treaty, McKelvey was the only IRA leader in Belfast to reject it, resigning his post as commandant of the Third Northern Division and joining the Republican Army Executive in Dublin. He was an occupant of the Four Courts from April to June 1922. After the fall of the building, he was arrested and held in Mountjoy Jail, where he, Rory O'Connor, Dick Barrett and Liam Mellows were executed on the morning of 8 December 1922.

Liam Mellows (1892–1922) was born in Ashton-under-Lyme, Lancashire, where his father served as a soldier in the British Army. Three years later, the family moved to Ireland, where Liam lived in Dublin, Wexford and Cork before settling in Dublin in 1904. He was educated at military schools in Cork and Dublin but did not join the army, instead finding work as a clerk. In 1911, he joined Fianna Éireann and in 1913 became a full-time organiser. In 1912, he was sworn into the IRB, and the following year supported James Connolly during the lockout. In 1913, he was appointed to the provisional committee of the Irish Volunteers; after the split the following year, he was sent to Galway to rebuild the organisation there. During the Easter Rising, he led a minor insurrection in the county. Having escaped to America, he returned to Ireland in 1919 having been appointed as Director of Arms Purchases for the IRA. Having been elected MP and latterly TD for Galway, he opposed the Treaty and lost his seat in the 'pact' election. A member of the Republican Army Executive, he sought to prevent the onset of war in May and June 1922, before occupying the Four Courts. After the fall of the building, he was arrested and imprisoned in Mountjoy Jail. While in prison he was appointed Minister for Defence in a Republican government, and conducted classes in socialism and socialist thinking, including the works of James Connolly, for left-wing Republicans, including Peadar O'Donnell. A surviving manuscript of his notes made in Mountjoy was posthumously published. He was executed along with O'Connor, McKelvey and Barrett on the morning of 8 December 1922.

Richard Mulcahy (1886–1971) was born in Waterford and worked as a post office clerk. During the Easter Rising, he was involved at an ambush at Ashbourne and by the end of the War of Independence he was IRA chief-of-staff. He supported the Treaty and sought to delay a split in the army for several months. He supported Michael Collins in his efforts to avoid a war, while also becoming chief-of-staff of the new National Army. After Collins' death, he became Minister for Defence and commander-in-chief of the Army. Following the end of the Civil War Mulcahy continued as minister until the 'Army Mutiny' of 1924 (when a group of National Army officers called for the disbandment of the military council, the governing body of the Army). In the wake of the mutiny Mulcahy resigned. In 1927, he was appointed Minister for Local Government and Public Health, serving until 1932. Following the foundation of Fine Gael in 1933 Mulcahy served on its executive and Dáil front bench, succeeding Cosgrave as leader in 1944. In 1948, he stood aside in favour of John A. Costello when the first Inter-Party government was formed, serving as Minister for Education from 1948 to 1951 and again from 1954 to 1957. He resigned as leader in 1959 and retired as a TD in 1961.

Kate (Murphy) O'Callaghan (1885–1961) was born near

Lissarda, Co. Cork, and educated in Dublin. In 1912 she moved to Limerick and succeeded her sister Mary as a senior lecturer in education at Mary Immaculate College (MIC). In 1914 she married Michael O'Callaghan, who became Mayor of Limerick in 1920; the following year he was assassinated by Crown forces. Kate was elected to Dáil Éireann later that year and opposed the Treaty. She was re-elected at the 'pact' general election in 1922 and worked to undermine the new Free State. A founding member of the WPDL, she was arrested in January 1923, being released later that year. Defeated in the general election of August 1923, she returned to Limerick. The following year she rejoined the staff of MIC as a supervisor of student teachers in the city. She opposed the 1937 Constitution, seeing it as a blow against the women's movement in Ireland. Until her death in March 1961, she was an active member of the cultural life of Limerick.

Rory O'Connor (1883–1922) was born in Dublin and educated at Clongowes and UCD, graduating BA (1906) and BEng (1911). After some time working in Canada, he returned to Dublin, working with Dublin Corporation. He was active in the Gaelic League and Irish Volunteers, and in 1916 was involved with Joseph Plunkett and his brother in producing the 'Castle document'. Having been sworn into the IRB, he resigned from the brotherhood in the wake of the Rising, having become convinced that secret societies were ineffective in the contemporary political environment. He joined the Volunteer GHQ in 1918 as Director of Engineering and after 1919 worked as the clerk of Dáil Éireann. After the Treaty split, O'Connor was to the forefront of the anti-Treaty IRA members. He was elected to the Republican Army Executive and was part of the force that occupied the Four Courts. After its fall, he was imprisoned in Mountjoy Jail, and was executed along with Barrett, McKelvey and Mellows on the morning of 8 December 1922.

Paddy O'Daly (1888–1957) was born in Dublin and educated in Clontarf, being apprenticed to a carpenter in Fairview. Having qualified as a carpenter, he worked in Galway, where he joined the Irish Volunteers and Fianna Éireann, as well as being sworn into the IRB. He was prominent in the Howth gunrunning in 1914 and during the Easter Rising, he led a raid on the Magazine Fort in the Phoenix Park. After his arrest and release, he became active in the reorganisation of the Republican movement in Dublin. In September 1919, he became part of Collin's 'Squad', and conducted several operations in the city during the War of Independence. In late 1921, he assumed command of the Dublin Guards (formed after a merger of a GHQ squad and the Dublin Brigades' active service unit). Following Collins, O'Daly supported the Treaty. The Dublin Guard became part of the new National Army and fought in Dublin and Kerry during the Civil War. Following the Army Mutiny O'Daly resigned his commission and returned to working as a building contractor. He re-enlisted in the Defence Forces during The Emergency before returning to the building trade.

Kevin O'Higgins (1892–1927) was born in Stradbally, Co. Laois, and was educated in Portlaoise, Clongowes, Maynooth and UCD. He joined Sinn Féin and the Irish Volunteers despite his brothers serving in the British Army in the First World War. In 1918, he was arrested and jailed for disturbing the peace. At the general election that year, he was elected MP for Queen's County (Laois); he sat in the First Dáil and became Assistant Minister for Local Government. Re-elected in 1921, he turned down the chance to be part of the London delegation to get married. He accepted the Treaty and became well-known for his strident defence of the settlement. At the outbreak of the Civil War, he was assistant to the adjutant general of the National Army. Following Collins' death, he became Minister for Home Affairs and later vice-president of the Executive Council. He was the public face of the regime and seen as the 'hard man' of Cosgrave's government. Following the end of the war, he continued his stance. On 10 July 1927, he was assassinated in Booterstown, Co. Dublin.

Ernie O'Malley (1897–1957) was born in Castlebar and was active in the IRA during the War of Independence. At the outbreak of the Civil War, he was assistant chief-of-staff in the anti-Treaty IRA. In October

1922, he was appointed to the Army Council, and was spectacularly arrested the following month. During his incarceration in Mountjoy Jail, he took part in the hunger strike; his frail health because of this led to his death sentence being commuted. Released in 1924, he spent most of the rest of his life abroad. His memoir of the Civil War, *The Singing Flame* (1978) is regarded as a classic account.

Grace (Gifford) Plunkett (1888–1955) was born in Rathmines and educated locally and in the Slade School of Art in London. On her return to Ireland in 1908 she became acquainted with Thomas MacDonagh and Pádraig Pearse, joining Inighinidhe na hÉireann. She worked as an illustrator for several newspapers and journals, producing artwork for the Irish Women's Franchise League. In 1915 she and Joseph Plunkett were engaged; a few hours before he was executed in May 1916, the pair married in Kilmainham Jail. The following year she was elected to the Sinn Féin executive, and produced banners, posters, and handbills for the movement. She opposed the Treaty and worked with the Women's Prisoners Defence League. In 1923 she was arrested and detained in Kilmainham, where she produced the 'Kilmainham Madonna' on the wall of her cell. Upon her release, she eschewed politics and worked in the Abbey Theatre as a costume designer. In 1934 she joined the Old Dublin Society. She died in 1955.

Jennie Wyse Power (1858–1941) was born in Baltinglass,

Co. Wicklow. Her life encompassed many strands ranging from the Land League to Sinn Féin. By the end of the War of Independence, she was a prominent leader of Cumann na mBan and joint treasurer of Sinn Féin. Supporting the Treaty, she founded Cumann na Saoirse and joined Cumann na nGaedheal; she resigned from the latter in 1925 having become disillusioned with the party's social and economic policies, and after the collapse of the Boundary Commission. As a member of the Free State Senate, she was a vociferous opponent of the government in relation to the status of women in the new state.

Hannah Sheehy-Skeffington (1877–1946) by the time of the Civil War was a veteran activist for women, Director of Organisation for Sinn Féin, and an executive committee member of the Irish White Cross. After the Treaty vote, which she opposed, she toured America raising funds for the families of Republican prisoners. Upon her return to Ireland, she co-founded the WDPL. Later in 1923 she was an unsuccessful delegate to the League of Nations against recognition of the Irish Free State.

Liam Tobin (1895–1963) was born in Cork City and educated in Kilkenny. Moving to Dublin to work as a clerk in 1912, he joined the Irish Volunteers and the IRB, serving in the Four Courts during the Easter Rising. After his release from prison, he worked closely with Michael Collins to reorganise the Volunteer movement. During the War of Independence, he served as an intelligence officer for IRA GHQ in Dublin. Tobin supported the Treaty, becoming a major-general in the National Army. Following Collins' death, he became aide-de-camp for Governor-General Tim Healy. In 1924, he was a leading member of the 'Army Mutiny' (when a group of National Army officers called for the disbandment of the military council, the governing body of the Army) which saw the effective death of the IRB as a legitimate force in Irish nationalist politics. Having resigned his commission, he worked in several jobs before joining Joe McGrath at the Irish Hospitals Sweepstake Company.

Oscar Traynor (1886–1963) was born in Dublin and trained as a wood carver and compositor. During the War of Independence, he led the abortive IRA attack on the Customs House on 25 May 1921. He opposed the Treaty and in the early weeks of the Civil War fought a stubborn resistance in Dublin and Wicklow. After the war, he remained a member of Sinn Féin until approximately 1929, when he joined Fianna Fáil. He served as a TD for several Dublin constituencies from 1932 until 1961 and as a minister in several De Valera-led governments. He was a noted soccer player in his youth, playing for teams in Dublin and Belfast. From 1948 until his death, he served as president of the Football Association of Ireland, and the trophy for an annual countrywide junior league competition bears his name.

APPENDIX

ÓGLAIĠ na hÉIREANN
Draft Constitution and Rules

1. The Army shall be known as the Irish Republican Army.
2. It shall be on a purely Volunteer Army basis.
3. Its objects shall be: –
   (a) To guard the honour and maintain the independence of the Irish Republic.
   (b) To protect the rights and liberties common to the people of Ireland.
   (c) To place its services at the disposal of an established Republican Government which faithfully upholds the above objects.

CONTROL OF THE ARMY
4. The Army shall be controlled by an executive of sixteen, which shall be appointed by a committee of twenty-five, selected as follows: –
   Each province elects five delegates.
   Each province nominates five further delegates from whom the whole convention will elect the remaining five. Any serving Volunteer to be eligible to act on the executive. This executive shall have supreme control of the Army, and the executive shall not itself, directly or indirectly, be subordinate to, or he controlled by any other body: Subject to any alterations necessary to put into operation section 3 (Sub-section (c) above. Such proposed alterations to be sanctioned by a general convention.

DUTIES AND POWERS OF EXECUTIVE
5. The duties of the executive shall be to define policy for the Army. It shall have supreme control over the Army Council and General Headquarters Staff. It shall not, however, have power to interfere with General Headquarters Staff in respect of purely Army matters, such as organisation, training, method of conducting operations, etc. Ten shall form a quorum at meetings of the executive.

FINANCIAL POWERS
6. The executive shall be responsible for and safeguarding of funds for Army purposes.

EXECUTIVE MEETINGS
7. The executive shall meet at least every two months. In the event of a vacancy occurring on the executive it shall be filled by co-option.

ARMY COUNCIL
8. The executive shall appoint an Army Council of seven, of which four shall be chosen from the members of the executive, and the remaining three may be appointed from outside the executive. Four shall form a quorum at meetings of the Army Council. In the event of a vacancy occurring on the council, it shall be filled by co-option to be approved by the executive.

GENERAL HEADQUARTERS STAFF
9. The executive shall appoint a Chief of Staff, who will appoint his staff.

GENERAL CONVENTION
10. A general convention representative of the whole Army shall meet at least once in each twelve months, and shall elect a committee to appoint an executive as in Section 4, who shall hold office until the next general convention. It shall also receive a report from the Chief of Staff, and a financial statement from the executive.

SYSTEM OF REPRESENTATION
11. The system of representation shall be as follows: –
At a company parade called for the purpose, one delegate shall be elected to attend a brigade convention where the number of men on parade does not exceed thirty men; two delegates where the number on parade is over thirty and under seventy men; three delegates where the number on parade exceeds seventy men; and an additional delegate for every thirty men over one hundred.
The election shall be by ballot.

BRIGADE CONVENTION

12. The constitution of the brigade convention shall be as follows: –

    (a) The brigade commandant and two members of his staff as elected by the staff.

    (b) Each battalion commandant and one member of his staff elected by the staff.

    (c) The company delegates as elected in accordance with the instructions detailed above.

    The staff in this connection shall be taken as including the officers commanding special services.

13. The brigade convention shall elect delegates to represent the brigade at the general convention. The number of delegates to be so elected shall be 5 per cent of the total number of delegates present at the brigade convention. In the event of such percentage resulting in a whole number and a fraction, the nearest whole number will be the number of delegates. The individual delegates so chosen need not necessarily be selected from those present at the convention, but must be active members of the brigade or of the staff of the division to which the brigade is attached.

GENERAL CONVENTION

14. The constitution of the general convention shall be as follows: –

    (a) All members of the executive.

    (b) All members of the Army Council.

    (c) All members of the General Headquarters Staff.

    (d) All divisional commandants, and two other members of the divisional staff as elected by that staff.

    (e) The delegates selected at the brigade convention.

VOTING AT CONVENTION

15. Voting on motions shall be carried out as decided by the chairman of the convention.

16. The chairman of the general convention shall be chosen by the convention.

QUORUM

17. The number to form a quorum at a general convention shall be

two-thirds of the total number of delegates entitled to attend.

EXTRAORDINARY CONVENTION
18. An extraordinary convention shall be called if required.
    (a) By a two-thirds majority of the executive.
    (b) By a two-thirds majority of G.H.Q.
    (c) By a two-thirds majority of the divisional commandants, provided they represent two-thirds of the total strength of the whole Army.

MEMBERSHIP OF ARMY
19. Only such persons shall be allowed to remain in, or shall be admitted to the Army who take the oath of allegiance to the Irish Republic. No person holding any rank in any other Army shall be enrolled in the Irish Republican Army.

20. The oath of allegiance to be taken by every member of the Army shall be as follows: –

> I, …….., do solemnly swear that to the best of my knowledge and ability I will support and defend the Irish Republic against all enemies foreign and domestic that I will bear true faith and allegiance to the same. I do further swear that I do not, and shall not, yield a voluntary support to any pretended government, authority, or power within Ireland hostile or inimical to that Republic. I take this obligation freely without any mental reservation or purpose of evasion so help me God.

AMENDING OF CONSTITUTION
21. It shall require a majority of two-thirds of the general convention to amend any article of the constitution.

Source: Florence O'Donoghue's *No Other Law*, Anvil Books, 1986.

BIBLIOGRAPHY

Borgonovo, John: *The Battle for Cork: July–August 1922* (Cork, 2011)

Burke, John: *Athlone 1900–1923: politics, revolution & civil war* (Dublin, 2015)

Coleman, Marie: *County Longford and the Irish Revolution* (Dublin, 2002)

Crowley, John, Ó Drisceoil, Donal and Murphy, Mike (eds.): *Atlas of the Irish Revolution* (Cork, 2017)

Deasy, Liam: *Brother against Brother* (Cork, reprinted 1994)

Doyle, Tom: *The Civil War in Kerry* (Cork, 2008)

— *The Summer Campaign in Kerry* (Cork, 2010)

Dorney, John: *The Civil War in Dublin: the fight for the Irish capital 1922–1924* (Sallins, Co. Kildare, 2017)

Durney, James: *The Civil War in Kildare* (Cork, 2011)

Dwyer, T. Ryle: *Tans, Terror and Troubles: Kerry's Real Fighting Story 1913–23* (Cork, 2001)

— *'I Signed My Death Warrant': Michael Collins & The Treaty* (Cork, 2006)

— *Michael Collins and the Civil War* (Cork, 2012)

Enright, Seán: *The Irish Civil War: law, execution and atrocity* (Newbridge, Co. Kildare, 2019)

Farry, Michael: *The Irish Revolution, 1912–23: Sligo* (Dublin, 2012)

— *The aftermath of revolution: Sligo, 1921–23* (Dublin, 2000)

Ferriter, Diarmaid: *Between Two Hells: The Irish Civil War* (London 2021)

Foster, Gavin: *The Irish Civil War and society: politics, class ad conflict* (New York, 2015)

Gillis, Liz: *The Fall of Dublin: 28 June to 5 July 1922* (Cork, 2011)

Glennon, Kieran: *From Pogrom to Civil War: Tom Glennon and the Belfast IRA* (Cork, 2013)

Harrington, Niall C.: *Kerry Landing* (Tralee, 1992)

Hart, Peter: *The I.R.A. at war, 1916–1923* (Oxford, 2003)

Hopkinson, Michael: *Green against Green: The Irish Civil War* (Dublin, 2004)

Keane, Barry: *Massacre in West Cork: the Dunmanway and Ballygroman Killings* (Cork, 2014)

Kenny, Colum: *Midnight in London: The Anglo-Irish Treaty Crisis 1921* (Dublin, 2021)

Kenny, Tomás: *Galway: politics and society 1910–23* (Dublin. 2011)

Laffan, Michael: *The Resurrection of Ireland: the Sinn Féin Party 1916–1923* (Cambridge, 1999)

Macardle, Dorothy: *The Irish Republic* (Dublin, 2005)

— *Tragedies of Kerry* (Tralee, 1937)

McCarthy, Brian: *The Civic Guard Mutiny* (Cork, 2012)

McCarthy, Cal: *Cumann na mBan and the Irish Revolution* (Cork, 2014)

McCarthy, John P.: *Kevin O'Higgins: Builder of the Irish State* (Dublin, 2006)

McCarthy, Pat: *The Irish Revolution, 1912–23: Waterford* (Dublin, 2015)

Neeson, Eoin: *The civil war in Ireland, 1922–23* (Cork, 1969)

Ó Duibhir, Liam J.: *Donegal and the Civil War: The Untold Story* (Cork, 2011)

O'Callaghan, John: *The Battle for Kilmallock* (Cork, 2011)

O'Malley, Ernie: *The Singing Flame* (Dublin, reprinted 1978)

Ó Ruairc, Pádraig Óg: *The Battle for Limerick City* (Cork, 2010)

— *Truce: Murder, Myth and the last days of the Irish War of Independence* (Cork, 2016)

Regan, John M.: *The Irish Counter-Revolution 1921–1936* (Dublin, 1999)

Ryan, Meda: *Tom Barry: IRA Freedom Fighter* (Cork, 2005)

— *The Real Chief: Liam Lynch* (Cork, 2005)

Townshend, Charles: The republic: the fight for Irish independence, 1918–1923 (London, 2014)

Younger, Calton: *Ireland's Civil War* (London, 1968)

INDEX

A

Adamson Castle 83
Ahiohill 88
Aiken, Frank 43, 44, 48, 52, 58, 79, 85, 87
Altnaveigh 42
Andrews, Todd 44, 62
Anti-Treaty Republicans 20, 22, 23, 24, 26, 28, 32, 33, 34, 35, 36, 38, 39, 40, 41, 42, 43, 44, 45, 46, 47, 48, 50, 51, 53, 54, 58, 59, 71, 72, 78, 79, 80, 94, 95, 99, 100, 109, 110
Ardnaree 52
Arigna Mountains 71
Armagh 42, 43, 87, 91
Army Council 64, 67, 80, 111
Army Emergency Powers Resolution (AEPR) 46, 64, 65, 66, 68, 80
Army Mutiny 107, 109, 113
Arnott, John 49
Ashbourne 107
Athlone 26, 40, 45, 46, 53, 54, 55, 82, 102

B

Baldonnel 70
Ballaghaderreen 83
Ballina 40, 41, 52, 72
Ballinamore 72
Ballinasloe 39
Ballineen 87
Ballingarry 52
Ballinrobe 40
Ballyconnell 71, 72
Ballycotton 24
Ballyheigue 65, 79
Ballymacarbery 57
Ballymore 54
Ballymote 53
Ballymullen Barracks 74, 76, 77, 79
Ballyseedy Woods 74, 76, 77, 78, 79
Ballyshannon 42
Ballyvourney 38
Baltimore 81
Baltinglass 111
Bandon 26, 73
Banna strand 79
Bantry 51, 80
Barrett, Dick 67, 105, 109
Barrinang Wood 75
Barry, Dinny 85
Barry, Tom 15, 22, 23, 26, 50, 55, 56, 57, 88
Barton, Robert 10, 11, 13, 14, 65, 88, 89
Beál na Bláth 38, 90
Belfast 10, 19, 42, 105, 113
Bennett, Louisa ('Louie') 32, 88
Better Government of Ireland Act 1920 10, 19
Birr 46
Blythe, Annie 21
Blythe, Ernest 21
Bofin, Ned 72
Bohola 40

Boundary Commission 12, 45, 112
Bray 93
Brennan, Michael 22, 23, 35
Brennan's Glen 63, 64
Breslin, Ned 78
Brideswell 54
Brosnan, Terry 77
Bruff 36
Brugha, Cathal 9, 13, 15, 16, 31, 33, 34, 99
Bruree 36
B Specials 42, 105
Buncrana 42
Byrne, Archbishop Edward 32
Byrne, Martin 70

C

Cahirciveen 74, 75, 78, 79
Callan 50, 51
Carnmore 39
Carolan, Michael 62
Carrick-on-Shannon 72
Carrick-on-Suir 51
Carty, Frank 55
Cashel 56
Cassidy, Peter 65
Castlebar 40, 41, 110
Castleisland 63
Castlemaine 74, 79
Castlemartyr 73
Cavan 45, 71, 72, 97
Chartres, John 14
Childers, Erskine 10, 11, 13, 14, 65, 66, 89, 101
Churchill, Winston 12, 28
Civic Guard 46, 81
Clann na Poblachta 90, 99

Clare 22, 27, 45
Claremorris 40
Clarke, Kathleen (Daly) 17, 89
Clarke, Tom 17
Clifden 39
Clifford, Madge 33
Clonakilty 27
Clonmel 21, 22, 36, 50, 101
Coachford 63
Cobh 24
Collins, Michael 9, 10, 11, 12, 13, 14, 16, 17, 19, 20, 26, 27, 28, 37, 38, 39, 42, 44, 46, 60, 62, 65, 69, 90, 92, 93, 107, 109, 110, 112
Comerford, Mary Eva (Máire) 21, 33, 49, 84, 91
Connacht 39, 40, 71, 79, 81, 82, 93
Connell, Dennis 77
Connolly, Ina 33
Connolly, Nora 33
Cope, Alfred 97
Cork 15, 23, 26, 28, 35, 36, 37, 38, 40, 51, 56, 63, 71, 72, 73, 77, 79, 80, 85, 87, 88, 90, 91, 93, 94, 100, 103, 106, 108, 112
Corrigan, M.A. 49
Corrigan, William 49
Cosgrave, W.T. 19, 47, 49, 51, 58, 64, 66, 67, 68, 69, 84, 91, 92, 107, 110
Costello, John A. 107
Countess Bridge 78, 79
Courtown 91
Criminal Investigation Department (CID) 60, 62
Crofts, Tom 56, 57

Culhane, Seán 31
Cull, Michael 71
Cumann na mBan 20, 21, 27, 33, 90, 91, 99, 100, 101, 103, 104, 105, 112
Cumann na nGaedheal 92, 103, 112
Cumann na Saoirse 21, 27, 49, 85, 112
Curragh 45, 69, 82, 102
Custume Barracks 46, 54, 82, 83

D

Dáil Éireann 10, 11, 13, 14, 15, 16, 17, 18, 19, 20, 21, 23, 24, 25, 46, 50, 62, 64, 67, 68, 71, 72, 88, 90, 92, 94, 95, 96, 97, 98, 105, 107, 108, 109, 110
Dalton, Charlie 61, 62
Dalton, Emmet 38, 61, 73, 92
Daly, Charlie 43
Daly, David 54
Daly, Edward 90
Davitt, Cahir 62, 93
Deane, Det. Tony 61
Deansgrange 90
Deasy, Liam 31, 51, 54, 55, 56, 94
Derrig, Tom 60
Derry 42
Despard, Charlotte 84, 101
De Valera, Éamon 10, 11, 15, 16, 17, 18, 19, 23, 26, 31, 47, 58, 65, 87, 88, 94, 95, 96, 97, 98, 101, 104, 113
Document No. 2 18
Dominion Status 13, 16

Donegal 27, 41, 42, 43, 70, 80
Down 91
Dowra 72
Dublin 9, 12, 13, 14, 15, 16, 20, 22, 24, 26, 28, 30, 31, 32, 33, 34, 35, 39, 47, 48, 49, 50, 55, 56, 59, 65, 66, 69, 72, 74, 75, 76, 78, 80, 84, 88, 89, 90, 91, 92, 93, 94, 95, 96, 97, 98, 99, 100, 101, 102, 104, 105, 106, 108, 109, 110, 111, 112, 113
Dublin Brigade 25
Duffy, George Gavan 11, 13, 21, 65, 68, 96
Duffy, Louise Gavan 21
Duggan, Eamonn 11, 14, 50, 95, 97
Duggan, Fr Tom 56
Dundalk 43, 101
Dun Laoghaire 39
Dunne, Michael 75
Dwyer, Seamus 49

E

Easter Rising 10, 91, 92, 94, 95, 97, 103, 106, 107, 109, 112
Executions 26, 48, 56, 59, 61, 65, 66, 67, 68, 69, 70, 71, 73, 79, 80, 81, 86, 87, 89, 90, 97, 105, 107, 109, 111
Executive Council 66, 67, 80, 92, 94, 96, 110
External association 13, 18

F

Fahereen 54
Farranfore 78
Fenit 36, 79, 98

Fermoy 100, 101
Fianna Éireann 61, 105, 106, 109
Fianna Fáil 58, 87, 88, 90, 94, 100, 102, 105, 113
Fifth Northern Division 44
Finner Camp 42
First Southern Division (FSD) 22, 24, 56, 95, 100
First Western Division (FWD) 22, 23, 35
Fisher, James 65
Fitzgerald, Desmond 21
Fitzgerald, Mabel 21
Forde, Liam 22, 23
Four Courts 9, 25, 26, 28, 29, 31, 32, 33, 39, 42, 59, 60, 82, 87, 91, 98, 105, 106, 109, 112
Fourth Western Division 52
Free State 46, 47, 48, 49, 54, 55, 56, 57, 58, 59, 62, 66, 68, 69, 72, 81, 85, 92, 94, 96, 108, 112
Fuller, Stephen 77, 78

G

GAA 87, 94, 105
Gaelic League 87, 94, 99, 105, 108
Gaffney, John 65
Galtee Mountains 52
Galvin, Jack 64
Galway 39, 40, 52, 82, 106, 109
Gavan Duffy, George 14
Gaynor, Seán 52
General Headquarters (GHQ) 9, 22, 35, 59, 62, 87, 98, 109, 113

General Headquarters (IRA) 9
George, David Lloyd 10, 12, 13, 28, 88, 95
Glasnevin 39, 90, 97, 98, 105
Glenavy, Lord 49
Glen of Aherlow, 52
Gormanstown 82
Gort 39
Griffith, Arthur 10, 11, 12, 13, 14, 16, 18, 19, 23, 26, 27, 28, 32, 37, 44, 90, 92, 95, 97

H

Hales, Seán 48, 66
Hales, Tom 26
Harrington, Niall 36, 79, 98
Hartnett, Willie 77
Harty, Archbishop John 56, 57
Headford 52
Healy, Joe 52
Healy, Tim 61, 113
Helvick Head 23
Henderson, Leo 29, 50
Higgins, Dr Thomas 70
Hogan, Dan 72
House of Commons 12, 39
Humphreys, Sighle/Sheila (Mary Ellen) 21, 98, 99
Hunger strike 74, 83, 85, 91, 101, 111

I

Inighinidhe na hÉireann (INH). 100, 104, 111
IRA convention 21, 24, 25, 100
Irish National League 99
Irish Republican Army (IRA) 9, 10, 14, 15, 21, 22, 23, 24,

25, 26, 27, 31, 41, 42, 43, 45,
46, 47, 48, 50, 52, 55, 56, 57,
58, 60, 61, 62, 66, 71, 72, 79,
80, 83, 87, 88, 90, 91, 93, 94,
95, 98, 100, 102, 103, 104,
105, 106, 107, 109, 110, 113
Irish Republican Brotherhood
(IRB) 9, 10, 13, 15, 48, 49,
69, 89, 90, 93, 94, 95, 100,
102, 105, 106, 108, 109, 112,
113
Irish Trades Union Congress
(ITUC) 89
Irish Women's Franchise 100,
111
Irishwomen's Suffrage 88
Irish Women Workers' Union
89

J

Jacob, Rosamund 32, 99
Johnson, Thomas 32, 68

K

Kenmare 36, 79
Kennedy, Hugh 46
Kennefick, Timothy 63
Keogh, Comdt Tom 63
Kerry 27, 35, 36, 63, 65, 66, 69,
71, 74, 76, 77, 78, 79, 81, 88,
93, 98, 99, 101, 109
Kilchreest 39
Kildare 26, 33, 34, 35, 69, 70
Kilflynn 77
Kilgarvan 79
Kilkenny 26, 27, 34, 35, 50, 92,
112
Killarney 26, 63, 64, 78, 79

Killorglin 64, 74, 76, 88
Kilmainham Gaol 25, 70, 74,
82, 84, 85, 99, 111
Kilmallock 36
Kiltimagh 52
Kiltoom 54
Kingsbridge 31
King's County (Offaly) 35, 70
KnockmealdownMountains 57,
101
Knocknagoshel 75, 78, 79

L

Lacey, Denis 21, 52
Lacken, Paddy Ryan 52
Laois (Leix) 35, 110
Larkin, Delia 33
Lawlor, Brig.-Gen. 83
Lawlor, Jack 65
Leahy, Mick 51
Lehane, Seán 43
Leinster 50, 82, 94
Leitrim 27, 72, 103
Liffey, River 29, 31, 33
Limerick 22, 23, 27, 35, 36, 52,
63, 81, 89, 98, 100, 108
Lisavaird 90
Lisburn 105
Lissarda 108
Liverpool 90
Lixnaw 77
Logue, Card. Michael 44
London 11, 13, 14, 16, 20, 23,
27, 28, 88, 89, 90, 93, 95, 96,
97, 103, 104, 110, 111
Longford 45, 54, 55, 102, 103
Lough Bofinna 80
Louth 43, 44, 81, 91, 95, 101

Luzio, Mons. 57
Lynch, Fionán 50
Lynch, Liam 22, 24, 25, 31, 35, 36, 38, 44, 50, 51, 55, 56, 59, 66, 95, 100
Lyons, Timothy 'Aeroplane' 77, 79

M

Macardle, Dorothy 76, 84, 101
MacBride, Maud Gonne 32, 84, 96, 100, 101
MacBride, Seán 25
Mac Eoin, Seán 15
MacEoin, Seán 15, 45, 46, 54, 83, 93, 102
MacNeill, Brian 41
MacNeill, Eoin 16, 41
Macroom 51, 63
MacSwiney, Anne 74
MacSwiney, Mary 16, 21, 28, 29, 84, 85, 103
MacSwiney, Terence 16, 103
Mahony, Paddy 77
Mallin, Joseph 66
Mallow 24, 31, 35, 81
Mannion, Patrick 61
Manorhamilton 72
Markievicz, Countess 21, 32, 101, 104
Mayo 27, 40, 41, 52, 63
McCarthy, Ben 80
McCullough, Denis 49
McDunphy, Michael 48
McElligot, John 77
McGarrity, Joseph 47
McGarry, Seán 48, 50
McGrath, Joe 50, 113

McGrath, Seán 71
McKelvey, Joe 67, 68, 105, 107, 109
Meath 82, 95, 100
Mellows, Liam 25, 40, 67, 87, 99, 105, 106, 109
Mid-Limerick Brigade 22
Moloney, Con 52
Moran, William 40
Morrissey, Patrick 83
Mountjoy Jail 32, 48, 49, 55, 68, 81, 84, 85, 87, 91, 93, 95, 97, 99, 101, 105, 106, 107, 109, 111
Moylan, Con 31
Moylan, Seán 31, 51
Mulcahy, Richard 9, 17, 21, 24, 32, 39, 46, 49, 64, 67, 68, 69, 72, 75, 78, 107
Mullaney, Patrick 70
Mullinavat 51
Mullingar 54
Mulrennan, Capt. Patrick 83
Munster 34, 36, 37, 39, 42, 50, 51, 93, 103
Munster Republic 37
Murphy, Bartholomew 63, 64
Murray, Patrick 51, 73

N

National Army 29, 31, 32, 33, 34, 35, 36, 38, 39, 40, 41, 42, 43, 44, 45, 46, 48, 50, 51, 52, 53, 54, 55, 59, 60, 61, 62, 63, 64, 65, 69, 70, 71, 72, 73, 74, 75, 78, 79, 80, 81, 82, 83, 84, 90, 93, 94, 98, 101, 102, 107, 109, 110, 113

Neutral IRA 56
Newcastle 57
Newcestown 73
Newport 41, 52
Newtown-Forbes 55
Northern Ireland 12, 26, 28, 41, 42, 43, 44

O

O'Callaghan, Kate 21, 28, 29, 84, 85, 107
O'Callaghan, Michael 108
O'Connell, J.J. 'Ginger' 29
O'Connor, Lieut P. 75
O'Connor, Rory 22, 23, 24, 25, 28, 29, 31, 67, 105, 107, 108
O'Daly, Brig. Gen. Paddy 64, 74, 75, 78, 109
O'Donoghue, Florence 56
O'Donovan, Dan ('Sandow') 23
O'Duffy, Eoin 24, 31, 75
O'Hegarty, Seán 23, 56
O'Higgins, Brigid 21
O'Higgins, Kevin 21, 46, 58, 67, 69, 70, 85, 110
O'Leary, Seamus 73
Omagh 44
Ó Máille, Pádraic 48, 66
O'Malley, Ernie 22, 23, 25, 32, 33, 43, 44, 45, 55, 84, 99, 110
O'Mara, Stephen 22
Ó Muirthuile, Seán 82
Operating Order No. 19 38
Oriel House 60, 61, 62, 85
O'Shea, D. 77
O'Sullivan, Andy 85
O'Sullivan, Gearóid 62
Ovens, William 71

P

Pender, Michael 54
Pettigo 42
Plenipotentiaries 11, 88
Plunkett, Count George 10
Plunkett, Grace Gifford 84, 111
Plunkett, Sir Horace 49
Portobello Barracks 65, 70
Power, Jennie Wyse 21, 49, 111
Price, Comdt-Gen. Eamon 51
Prisoners 50, 55, 56, 63, 64, 66, 68, 69, 73, 74, 75, 76, 77, 78, 79, 80, 81, 82, 83, 84, 85, 86, 97, 101, 112
Pro-Treaty 17, 18, 19, 20, 22, 26, 27, 28, 29, 37, 60, 61, 66, 89, 92
Provisional Government 20, 21, 26, 32, 33, 37, 38, 41, 42, 43, 44, 46, 59, 60, 81, 82, 90, 92, 96

R

Railroad Protection and Maintenance Corps (RPMC 81
Railways 53, 69, 72, 81
Raphoe 42
Rathbride 69
Rathdrum 91
Red Cow 61
Republican Army Executive (RAE) 25, 28
Republican government 9, 47, 106
Republican IRA 21, 22, 23, 25, 26, 27, 31, 32, 62
Reynolds, David 73
Ring, Brig.-Gen. Joe 41

Robinson, Seamus 22, 23
Roscommon 27, 41, 46, 71, 98
Rossadrehid 52
Rosscarbery 88
Rosslare 81
Ruane, Tom 40
Ruttledge, P.J. 31
Ryan, J.T. ('Jetter') 57
Ryan, Min 21, 49
Ryan, William 71

S

Saor Eire 99
Saurin, Frank 60
Schull 81
Second Southern Division
    (SSD) 22, 23
Shanahan, Dr 78
Sheehy, John Joe 78
Sheehy-Skeffington, Hannah
    32, 100, 112
Silvermines Mountains 52
Sinn Féin 9, 10, 11, 14, 18, 20,
    23, 26, 28, 42, 43, 58, 87,
    89, 90, 91, 92, 94, 96, 98, 99,
    100, 101, 104, 105, 110, 111,
    112, 113
Skibbereen 81
Sligo 40, 41, 45, 46, 52, 53, 55,
    63, 103, 104
Squad 60, 62, 63, 109
Stack, Austin 10, 15, 16, 57
Staines, Michael 46
Stapleton, Joseph 75
Stopford Green, Alice 91
Stradbally 70, 110
Sullivan, Pete 77
Swanzy, DI 105

Sweeney, Joe 43
Sweeney, Michael 26
Swinford 40

T

Thomastown 51
Tipperary 21, 27, 33, 35, 40, 47,
    50, 51, 52, 57, 63, 81, 98, 101
Tipperary Brigade 21
Tobin, Liam 31, 60, 112, 113
Tralee 64, 74, 75, 76, 98
Traynor, Oscar 22, 25, 32, 33,
    113
Treaty 11, 13, 14, 15, 16, 17, 18,
    19, 20, 21, 23, 27, 28, 44, 47,
    49, 56, 58, 87, 88, 90, 91, 92,
    93, 94, 95, 96, 97, 100, 102,
    103, 105, 106, 107, 108, 109,
    110, 111, 112, 113
Truce 9, 10, 60, 80, 88, 97
Tubbercurry 53
Tuomey, Timmie 77
Twohig, Richard 65
Twomey, Maurice ('Moss') 31,
    35, 41
Tyrone 42, 44, 105

U

Ulster 10, 39, 42, 43
Union Hall 36
Upnor 23, 24, 53
USA 57, 91

W

Walsh, J.J. 49
Warrior 23, 24
Waterford 23, 27, 35, 50, 51, 57,

81, 99, 100, 107
Western Command 45, 55, 102
Westmeath 45, 54, 80, 102
Westport 41, 52
Wexford 34, 80, 91, 106
Wicklow 34, 65, 88, 89, 91, 93,
   112, 113
Wilson, Sir Henry 28
Women's Prisoners Defence
   League (WPDL) 84, 100,
   108, 111, 112

Y

Youghal 36, 73